M000004967

100
answers to
100 questions

ask
discover
live smart

every
Graduate
should know

100
answers to
100 questions

ask · discover · live smart

every
Graduate
should know

Christian
LIFE
A STRANG COMPANY

Most CHRISTIAN LIFE products are available at special quantity discounts for bulk purchase for sales promotions, premiums, fund-raising, and educational needs. For details, write Christian Life, 600 Rinehart Road, Lake Mary, Florida 32746, or telephone (407) 333-0600.

100 Answers to 100 Questions Every Graduate Should Know

Published by Christian Life
A Strang Company
600 Rinehart Road
Lake Mary, Florida 32746

www.strang.com

This book or parts thereof may not be reproduced in any form, stored in a retrieval system, or transmitted in any form by any means—electronic, mechanical, photocopy, recording, or otherwise—without prior written permission of the publisher, except as provided by United States of America copyright law.

Scripture quotations marked HCSB are from the Holman Christian Standard Bible®, Copyright © 1999, 2000, 2002, 2003 by Holman Bible Publishers. Used by permission. Holman Christian Standard Bible®, Holman CSB ®, and HCSB ® are federally registered trademarks of Holman Bible Publishers.

Scripture quotations noted NAS are from the New American Standard Bible®, copyright © 1960, 1962, 1963, 1968, 1971, 1973, 1975, 1977, 1995 by The Lockman Foundation. Used by permission.

Scripture quotations marked NIV are from the Holy Bible, New International Version. Copyright © 1973, 1978, 1984, International Bible Society. Used by permission.

Scripture quotations marked NLT are from the Holy Bible, New Living Translation, copyright © 1996, 2004. Used by permission of Tyndale House Publishers, Inc., Wheaton, IL 60189. All rights reserved.

Cover design by Whisner Design Group, Tulsa, Oklahoma

Copyright © 2008 by GRQ, Inc.
All rights reserved

ISBN 10: 1-59979-479-9
ISBN 13: 978-1-59979-479-2

BISAC Category: Religion/Christian Life/General

First Edition

08 09 10 11 12—9 8 7 6 5 4 3 2 1

Printed in the United States of America

"I know the plans I have for you," declares the LORD, "plans to prosper you and not to harm you, plans to give you hope and a future."

Jeremiah 29:11, NIV

C o n t e n t s

The Communication Conundrum: Honing People Skills

Stop and Listen: What Is God Saying?

Optimistic Realism: Dealing with Failure

Dreams and Visions: Thinking Big No Matter What

The Graduate's Achilles' Heel: Dealing with Relationship Issues

Mirror, Mirror, on the Wall: A Closer Look at You

Harvest for Tomorrow: Investing Now for Personal Growth

The Big Question Mark:
When You Just Don't Know What to Do

Introduction

Starting from scratch is not always fun. Even when it is fun, it does not always feel safe. Of course, you have likely had several new beginnings in your lifetime already. After elementary school, you jumped to middle school. Then once you became the top dog in junior high, you again faced starting all over when you hit high school.

There is something attractive about familiarity. People often like to hang around people like themselves and around places they know well. Yet something deep within the human heart yearns for adventure and excitement. This is where you are. You have a blank slate and can choose any one of a million choices.

The limitless possibilities are some of the scariest aspects for a young person because the chances of making the wrong decision are increased. If there are only two options, you at least have a fifty-fifty chance of getting it right. Do not worry! Take a deep breath and count to ten before you hyperventilate. This book is practical, insightful, and designed to help you take this next leap.

Many young people fear making the wrong decision and do not allow themselves to really appreciate this new adventure that lies ahead. Here is a little secret to help take some pressure off: no one ever gets it right every single time.

If you want to be successful, you must realize that life is less about being perfect and never making mistakes and more about learning as you go and making adjustments. Many people do not know where to begin, however, so this book gives you a solid starting point. This book seeks to address vital aspects of life that you will face, aspects from choosing a roommate and dealing with possible relational issues to taking an introspective look at yourself.

If you want to start right, then keep on reading.

> *Who is wise and understanding among you?*
> *He should show his works by good conduct*
> *with wisdom's gentleness.*
>
> James 3:13, HCSB
>
> *The greatest use of life is to spend it for*
> *something that will outlast it.*
>
> William James

1 question

Are you taking time to cherish memories?

Turning final grades in, getting ready for graduation, and accepting all of the well wishes from your uncle Benny and aunt Gertrude consume your time, as well as keep you from finding time to plan for the next phase in your life. Before you know it, you will be forty-nine, have four kids, and be gearing up for retirement. That "time flies" is the most overstated understatement of all time. It is true, and it is important to reflect from time to time.

answer

If you do not take time to think about past memories, they can become fuzzy and sometimes forgotten altogether. You do not want that inspiring teacher to become What's-His-Name. Here are some guidelines to help you remember important memories:

Three favorite moments. Pinpoint the three favorite memories you have of your school years. One might be the time that special someone gave you that look. Alternatively, it might be when Mr. Whittaker slipped and fell in biology. There will be tough times ahead, but remembering these types of things can often give a boost when spirits are low.

One humbling moment. There are times when you succeed and others hold you in higher esteem than they ought. Remember a moment that helps keep you grounded. Maybe it was that time you gave a riveting speech and were overwhelmed by the applause of the audience only to find out later that you had toilet paper on your shoe.

Three important people. It is vital to acknowledge those who touched your life. You can save yourself a lot of pain by watching and learning from others. Maybe a teacher believed in you, or a best friend has always been loyal to you. Remember what you learned from them.

One infamous person. There are also people from whom you learn what not to do, people who think the world of themselves. Learning from the mistakes of others can save you much time and pain.

worth thinking about

▶ **Always focus** more on the positives than the negatives. Not-so-perfect memories can offer many lessons that you can learn from.

▶ **Give grace** to people who were less than the best models. As time goes on, they may change.

▶ **Keeping a journal** or photo album can be helpful for keeping memories intact. Now you can even keep videos in your iPod, cell phone, or computer.

> *For some life lasts a short while, but the memories it holds last forever.*
> Laura Swenson

question

Can you live in the here and now?

The human experience is often like a Chevy at NASCAR—rolling at two hundred miles per hour, rushing to get to the finish line, but letting many things pass by without notice. The pace of life does seem to pick up after graduation, so in your excitement (or panic) to get wherever it is that you are going, do not forget to live in the here and now. In other words, learn simply to be.

answer

Some people never let the past go. They choose to live in things they once did with friends they once had. Then one day the girl who used to be the homecoming queen wakes up to realize she is still waiting tables twenty years after her friends have all moved on. Some people have the opposite problem. They constantly worry about the future. They never rest. Their minds constantly mull over the forty-nine worst-case scenarios that begin with *What if?*

To live fully in the present, you have to adopt the traffic light principle: stop, slow, and go!

Stop. Stop worrying about what the future might bring. Worrying never helped anyone do anything. Stop thinking of the past. Cherishing memories is one thing, but do not let yourself be consumed with how great the past was—or how great your regrets are.

Slow. Slow down and rest. You just graduated! Take the time to enjoy sleeping in your bed. Notice the texture of your sheets or the birds outside your window. Enjoy the victory of completing school.

Go. Finally, go have fun. Simply enjoy being free of assignments. Go on a picnic or for a ride on a roller coaster. Attend a baseball game or go camping with friends. Taking advantage of the present is a healthy way to reward yourself for hard work and to recharge before you head off to the next stage of your life.

worth thinking about

▶ **The next time** you are out, do not worry about the traffic that is slowing your progress or the bad driver who just cut you off. Instead, notice the flowers in the field, the synergy at the local café, and the clouds against the blue sky.

▶ **While resting**, start a low-stress hobby such as photography or model railroading.

▶ **If you cannot** seem to stop worrying about all that is on your plate, go see a movie. Perhaps go swimming. Do something that requires your full attention.

> *The future hasn't happened yet, and the past is gone. So . . . I try to make the best of those moments, the moments that I'm in.*
> Annie Lennox

3 question

Are you planning for the future?

The Bible says not to worry about tomorrow, and many people may take this verse to mean something it does not. This verse warns against wasting time fretting. Planning and worrying, however, are not the same things. When you were in school and you had to take a test, it was important to actually study in order to do well. You did not need to get an ulcer living in fear of what you might not know, but you did need to be as prepared as possible.

answer

Put it this way: it isn't a bad idea to keep both eyes on the road, but occasionally you need to look up at the street signs so you know where you are going. New graduates often do not have a clue as to what the next step is. Many do not know that the answer to this issue is their GPA—goals, personality, and attributes.

Goals. What do you want to accomplish in your life? Sit down and make a list of all the stuff you would like to do if you could. Once you have compiled the list, organize the items into categories. For instance, if you have many places you would like to visit, list those under "Traveling." In addition, if you notice you have many relational goals like having kids and getting married, put those under "Family." This will not give you all the answers you want, but it will get you started on what kinds of things you want to do.

Personality. Everyone is different, so find out who you are. To do this you need to take a personality test such as the MBTI (Myers-Briggs Type Indicator) or the DISC (dominance, influence, steadiness, conscientiousness) assessment. These multiple-choice tests show your strengths and weaknesses and even suggest potential careers.

Attributes. Each individual has gifts and attributes, so notice what you have naturally to work with. Be realistic. If you are seven-feet-two, for instance, it is unlikely that you will be a jockey. If you are three-feet-four, it is unlikely that you will play center for the Detroit Pistons.

worth thinking about

▶ **When looking** over your list of goals, note which category is the longest. That category may be the key to identifying what you really want to do.

▶ **Many online** personality tests are available for you to take. Simply type "online personality tests" into a search engine. Be sure to take one that is free.

▶ **If you do not** know your natural abilities, ask someone like a parent or teacher whom you trust to be honest with you.

> *The plans of the diligent certainly lead to profit, but anyone who is reckless only becomes poor.*
> Proverbs 21:5, HCSB

4

question

What is your diploma actually worth?

The summer breeze brushes your brow. Smiles glisten as people look your way, and you hear a loud ovation as your name is called. The next thing you know you are back in your seat. It all went by so fast. You were so caught up in making sure you didn't trip that you almost forgot you walked across the stage and got your diploma. Now what? What can this piece of paper do for you?

answer

Now that you are a graduate and not a student, you face the cold reality of the real world. Your diploma is not a magic wand that you wave to conjure up cash and purpose. You must now use that brain you have been educating if you are to get where you want to go.

Having your diploma shows that you can finish something. Potential employers are attracted to people who can finish what they start. People who follow through on tasks are an endangered species in many offices across America. Having your diploma also shows you that you can accomplish your goals if you stick with them long enough and work hard. Graduating can build your confidence. Having confidence is not all you need to succeed, however. You also need to consider the quality of your diploma.

A key way to identify what your diploma is worth is to be aware of what you know. What do you remember? What have you forgotten? If the mathematical equations you learned two years ago seem less clear than a mud-filled swimming pool, your diploma probably will not be worth much in the engineering field. However, if you do well with grammar and words, your diploma might just help you do well as a book editor.

It is important to know that your diploma does not make you the best candidate for every job. Yet, it can definitely open doors if you target the right fields.

worth thinking about

▶ Employers place a high value on references, and your teachers can be good references if you have done well in class. Make sure you ask permission prior to listing anyone as a reference.

▶ Do not talk negatively about your school. If you do, you are demeaning your diploma and lessoning your own value.

▶ Be sure to highlight the positives of your education experience and to downplay the negatives. Negativity can make you look pessimistic.

> *An investment in knowledge always pays the best interest.*
> Benjamin Franklin

5 question

How do you deal with loneliness?

Starting over is never easy. This is especially true with regard to relationships. When your social circle is established, you know where you stand in your group. You know your friends, and they know you. When you ride in a car, you know who sits where. When you have to begin from scratch, it is easy to begin to feel lonely. What are you to do when loneliness sets in?

answer

Loneliness is a part of being human; everybody experiences it at some point. Do not think that you are alone in feeling lonely. The following is a list of things to do when you get lonely:

Recognize reasons you may be lonely. Loneliness can sometimes be God's sign that He wants more quality time with you. Spend some time reading the Bible or praying. If you have not tried this yet, give it a shot. It cannot hurt anything.

Hang out with people. Even if you are in a new place, go where people can be found, perhaps a coffee shop or a beach. Sometimes merely being around people can help lessen the feelings of loneliness.

Connect with someone else who could use a friend. This may mean calling someone you do not normally like hanging out with, like a rambunctious sibling. Human contact is important.

Embrace solitude. Sometimes it isn't such a bad idea to spend time alone. Reading, writing, relaxing, and enjoying some type of artistic expression like classical music can be rewarding. You may discover something new that you enjoy.

Get out and play. It can be easy, in a new situation, to slip off into the shadows and watch everything from the sidelines because it is safer and less threatening. Do not be afraid to be yourself around new people. They may not like you, but that is life. You will not have the approval of 100 percent of the people 100 percent of the time. However, if you do take a chance and gain a friend, the risk would be well worth it.

worth thinking about

▶ **While trying** to meet new people, it is important to be aware that relationships are not always equal. Do not settle for unpleasant or untrustworthy people as friends just because you are lonely.

▶ **Another way** to embrace solitude is to visit new places. Eat at a restaurant you have never been to or shop at a store you've been meaning to check out.

▶ **When you are** lonely, you are often self-focused, so determine to do something that helps someone else.

> *The most terrible poverty is loneliness,*
> *and the feeling of being unloved.*
> Mother Teresa

How important is the work ethic?

Even when we were with you,
we used to give you this order:
if anyone is not willing to work,
then he is not to eat, either.

2 Thessalonians 3:10, NAS

6

Why is community important?

Human interaction has been a staple of civilization all throughout history. From the early church to the modern universities in America, people have leaned on other people. No one person can do everything alone. Even superheroes need help. Just look at the Justice League: Superman is the heart; Batman is the brains; Wonder Woman adds a feminine touch; and The Flash adds the comedic humor. Community betters individuals.

answer

In comic books, sports, and even in business, teamwork lessons abound. The following is a list of reasons why community is important, whom you should commune with, and where you should go for community.

Why. Fight off loneliness by plugging into a community. Being connected gives a sense of belonging and purpose. Having friends comes in handy when something in your life goes wrong. Having people who support you in a time of crisis is invaluable.

Another good reason for plugging in is that when you isolate yourself, you tend to become content with your personal status quo. Being around other people stretches and challenges how you think. Introverts can gain from extroverts, men can learn from women, and Europeans can learn from Canadians. God gave each person a uniqueness to add a little richness to others.

Who. Community provides people who lift you up rather than pull you down. Surround yourself with people of high values. This does not mean that you never reach out to people who do not share what you believe, but it does mean that the core group of people you depend on should be solid.

Where. Church is a great place to connect with other people. Church people aren't perfect, but many studies confirm that those people who attend church regularly live a higher quality of life and have a higher sense of happiness overall. They must be doing something right.

worth thinking about

- ▶ **Having community** gives you a chance to give back to others. Living in isolation encourages a person to live a self-focused life.

- ▶ **Having community** that shares strong values will help you in hard times. For example, when you get married, lean on those who have a good record of accomplishment in relationships and not those who are pessimistic toward marriage.

- ▶ **Do not expect** the church to be full of perfect people. Regular, everyday people fill churches.

> *He who separates himself seeks his own desire, he quarrels against all sound wisdom.*
> Proverbs 18:1, NAS

question

How can men dress professionally?

First impressions are not always correct, but they are often decisive. Fair or not, people make judgments on how you look, so why not look nice? Some men are unable to keep up with the latest fashions because they do not have a lot of money. Others have the money, but they choose to dress down. Then there are the men who simply do not know how to look nice. This section focuses on how men should dress.

answer

The following are basic wardrobe guidelines for professional men:

Suits. You should have at least one solid-color suit, either navy or dark gray. One in each color would be even better. The suit should be neither too heavy nor too light so that you can wear it year-round. As you can afford it, add a pinstriped navy suit, a pinstriped gray suit, and a charcoal gray suit.

Sports jacket and trousers. Choose a navy sports jacket with gray trousers.

Dress shirts. White, light blue, and pinstriped are always good choices. Solid-color pastel colors are good, as are solid-color bright or vibrant colors as long as they are not neon.

Dress pants. Black, gray, brown, tan, and navy are good colors for your pants.

Shoes. Choose one pair of black slip-on shoes and one pair of black lace-up shoes. Brown would also be a good color to have.

Socks. You need several pairs of black socks for dress. Gray, brown, and navy are also good. Never white.

Ties. Solid-color ties are a safe choice. Also good are stripes and patterns, as long as they are not "cute."

Casual Fridays. Choose sports shirts with collars or banded necks or polo shirts with collars; for pants choose chinos or Dockers-style in khaki or light gray; and for shoes, choose loafers or lace-ups.

worth thinking about

▶ **Be careful** not to wear the pants of a suit without the jacket too often. After a while, the pants will fade and wear down to where they do not even match the jacket.

▶ **When going** to a job interview, always wear at least a sports jacket. If you are applying to a large corporation or for a management-level job, wear a suit. Avoid matching a dark navy jacket with black pants.

▶ **Your belt** should match the color of your shoes.

> *You never get a second chance to make a first impression.*
> Author Unknown

How can women dress professionally?

First impressions are not always correct, but they are often decisive. Fair or not, people make judgments on how you look. This can be even trickier for women than for men. Women have many more options when it comes to wardrobe. Expectations can also vary depending on the organization's culture. You want to dress professionally and yet be distinctly feminine. Here are some suggestions for the clothes you need to accomplish this.

answer

Business suits. You need two or three business suits in neutral colors, such as navy, gray, or black. A skirt with a blazer is also acceptable. Until you get a feel for your organizational culture, play it safe by wearing suits rather than dresses. Some studies indicate that a skirted suit is a safer choice for a first interview but that a pantsuit is acceptable for a second or third interview.

Blouses. Have at least five different blouses to go with your suits. You need at least one white or ivory shirt, and the rest can be neutrals or subtle colors. The more you can wear with your suits, the more options you have.

Black dress. A simple but elegant black dress is an absolute necessity. A matching jacket in the day will allow you to transition to evening when you remove it. Accessorize it with elegant and tasteful gold or pearl jewelry. Skirt length should be a little below the knee or at the knee.

Shoes. Invest in quality leather shoes, and keep them polished. Select comfortable but classic heel heights, eschewing flats with less than an inch-and-a-half heel.

Handbags. You should have at least one fine-quality handbag in a neutral color that will coordinate with your business wardrobe. Depending on the corporate climate, you may want to carry a briefcase instead of a purse.

Accessories. Avoid a costume-jewelry look, and choose classic, go-with-all pieces. You can wear simple gold earrings every day. Wear light makeup, and choose conservative colors for lips and nails. Panty hose or stockings should be a neutral beige, and not black or navy.

worth thinking about

▶ Be sure to wear panty hose or stockings and not go bare-legged.

▶ A good test for the length of a skirt is to make sure you can sit down and bend over without being immodest.

▶ Avoid low-cut necklines. You want people to know you for your body of work and not for your body. Cleavage is out of place in the office.

> *Like a gold ring in a pig's snout is a beautiful woman who shows no discretion.*
> Proverbs 11:22, NIV

question

Is personal fulfillment more important than money?

When you were in school, pressures came from all sides. Perhaps you wanted to be a ballplayer or cheerleader or even class president. The real question is not whether those were admirable goals; rather, the real question is whether they were your goals. You need to know what brings fulfillment into your life, because things are not altogether different outside of school. Many people, for instance, will try to influence you to seek wealth as the standard of fulfillment.

answer

You do not have to know exactly what you will do for the rest of your life, but you do need to know what you will not do. Ask yourself how important money is to you. Ask yourself what the cost will be to get the money you seek. For some people, living the simple life is more advantageous in the end. In the movie *Mr. Deeds*, Longfellow Deeds inherits a ton of money as well as an entire company. Deeds, who grew up in a simple town of simple people, was not accustomed to the stresses and impersonal business practices of leading a major company. He eventually gave up all the money because he grew tired of the lifestyle and relationships that went along with the wealth. In a strange turn of events, Deeds still ended up with a nice sum of cash (though not nearly as much as he had), and Longfellow Deeds bought brand-new cars for everyone in his whole town. He then decided to go after his dream of writing greeting cards.

Is being good at making money a bad thing? No, but it is not for everyone. You must ask yourself if it is for you. Mother Teresa is famous for giving up her possessions and dedicating her life to serving the needy people in Calcutta, India. What if she had decided instead to be a small-business owner? What would her life have been like? Having money is not innately wrong, but do not sell your personal fulfillment in exchange.

worth thinking about

▶ **Workaholics often** live a life focused on money. Hard work is one thing, but when life becomes work at the expense of others, then you might want to alter some things in your life.

▶ **It is possible** to fulfill yourself by doing good work if you have a knack for making money. However, your focus should be on God and not on money itself.

▶ **There are examples** of people in the Bible who were financially successful. For instance, it was Abraham's faith and not his money that God saw as "pleasing."

> *Whoever loves money never has money enough; whoever loves wealth is never satisfied with his income. This too is meaningless.*
> Ecclesiastes 5:10, NIV

question

How do you prepare for an interview?

Even if you plan to continue your education, you will likely need to get a job, and to do so you will need to prepare for the interviewing process. Most candidates win or lose the job in the interviewing stage. If a potential employer has scheduled you for an interview, the interviewer has likely already seen your résumé. You improve your chances if there is something on it that stands out. Here are some tips on how to prepare for an interview:

answer

Do your research. Be sure you know for which job you are interviewing. Know the specific field it is in and as much about the company as you can. Do your best to put yourself in the shoes of the one interviewing. What would he or she like to know?

Be honest with yourself. You need to know that you can actually do the job if the company offers it to you. Do you have the skills it takes to do a good job? If you are bad with math, interviewing for an accountant position is likely a waste of time. Can you get the job done? If not, why waste everyone's time?

Be precise. Focus on your top skills, and highlight where you excel. Most employers do not have time to listen to your entire life story, so make it easy for them by talking about relevant and recent accomplishments, and the best aspects of your work approach.

Focus on image. Image is not everything in life, but it is for an interview. You can never redo first impressions, so make sure you dress to impress. If you do not dress appropriately, it will be distracting. Do not let your clothes overshadow you.. For example, a female should not wear big jewelry, especially around the face, because she will want to direct the employer's focus to her rather than to her accessories. Be sure to smile and show confidence, because if you do not believe in yourself, it will be hard for anyone else to do so, either.

worth thinking about

▶ **Avoid wearing** clothes that have busy patterns. They put attention on what you are wearing instead of on you.

▶ **Avoid underselling** yourself. A job interview is a place to put your best foot forward. This does not mean to exaggerate, however.

▶ **Ask informed** questions during the interview. You, too, are evaluating whether the job is a good fit for you. Most interviewers welcome questions because they show genuine interest.

> *Every time you smile at someone, it is an action of love, a gift to that person, a beautiful thing.*
> Mother Teresa

question

Have you looked into jobs or new schools?

It is okay not to know exactly what you want to do the rest of your life. It is also okay to know precisely what it is that you want to do with your life. Yet if you do not take a step toward something, something terrible happens: nothing. Whether you are lost or you know exactly where you are going, if you stop, you will go nowhere.

answer

If your answer to the question is no, you have some work to do. Here are a few things you need to do to get back on track:

When. Apply now. You need to start looking for jobs or schools soon. Most schools have deadlines for applications from mid to late summer. Certain programs have a set limit so when spots run out, they do not accept anyone else. Many companies start their recruiting process in October or November of the previous year. Do not procrastinate in applying because you might be too late.

Why. You have just graduated. That is very exciting, and you do not want to lose your momentum. Besides, some places give you more grace when you are right out of school because they know you are fresh. If you wait three years to apply, they will want to know why you have wasted time.

How. You should start looking for jobs in the daily newspaper. Yes, people still post jobs in the paper. Craigslist.com is a new way to find jobs. You can look into many other Web sites as well. If you have no idea where to look, ask your friends where they are applying for schools and jobs. Many schools have a career adviser you can talk to in order to get advice.

Where. You need to make a list of places where you would like to work or continue your education. Make a list of seven to ten places that you are interested in and apply.

worth thinking about

▶ **Do not feel** as though you have to choose one or the other. You can choose to take a few classes on the side and work at the same time.

▶ **Applying does not** mean you are committing right at that very moment. It just allows you to see what your options are. You never know when something might present itself that you did not expect and that really excites you.

▶ **The first step** is often the hardest, so gather applications and fill them out as soon as possible.

It is easier to steer a moving ship.
Author Unknown

question

12

Should you continue your education?

According to the most recent U.S. census, 15 percent of adults over the age of twenty-five had undergraduate degrees; just over 9 percent had graduate degrees; and less than 1 percent had doctoral degrees. Because you have just finished school, you may not want to think just yet about studying, writing, and taking tests. However, there are benefits to furthering your education. Several studies indicate that on average the more education you have, the more money you are likely to make.

answer

Whether to further your education depends on you and your circumstances. Continuing your education rarely is a bad idea, but before you do, think these things over:

Does your field require it? If you are going into a field such as education or psychology, it is often required, and at the very least strongly advantageous, to further your education as much as possible. If you want to go into acting, however, an advanced degree does not necessarily help. Even in fields such as acting, you can always use your education to learn and perhaps even teach.

What is your financial situation? Many people do not want to spend money they do not have. You need to look into the costs of a program that interests you. When money is an issue, you should look into the grants and scholarships that may be available to you. You can get reasonable loans through the school's financial aid department. If you treat these loans as an investment and work hard to get good grades and learn all you can, then furthering your degree can enhance your earning power.

What do you have to lose? If you still do not know what you want to do with your life, do not feel alone. Many people do not have a clue what to do after graduation, so if you have a hunger to learn and there are no other blaring options, going back to school can be a good option for you.

worth thinking about

▶ **Furthering your education** does not automatically give you a higher-paying job. You still need to work hard and hone your skills.

▶ **Continuing your schooling** can enhance intellect and self-confidence. It can also help sharpen your social skills, because you will be learning with people who are different than you are.

▶ **Never graduate** from life. You should make yourself a student for life, that is, you should always be open to learning new things. A degree does not mean you know it all.

> *Let the wise listen to these proverbs and become even wiser. Let those with understanding receive guidance.*
>
> Proverbs 1:5, NLT

13 question

How will you pay the bills?

There are questions that strike passion into a person's heart, such as "Do you love me?" There are questions that incite a cerebral debate in one's mind, such as "What is the meaning of life?" Then there are questions that are not so exciting, such as "How will you pay the bills?"

answer

Paying your bills is a part of everyday life. There is no way to get around it, at least not legally. Paying bills goes right along with breathing, eating, and sleeping. The following is a list of true and false assumptions about bills:

If I pray or wish hard enough, my bills will do me a favor and pay themselves. False. Bills do not simply disappear. You must accept the cold, hard truth that you have a responsibility to spend money on things you would rather not, things like power and water. Having a job is not a luxury; it is a necessity. If your job does not cover your bills, find a better job or cut your bills down.

Setting a budget is a good idea. True. Setting up a budget is not like going to the dentist. It is far more painful to regret not having done so than to do the work in the first place. First, you must add up all of your bills for a month and compare them to how much you make in a month. This gives you an idea of how much you need each month to pay bills. Figure out how much of the money left over you want to save, invest, and spend. Keep a close eye on all your finances.

Having a bank account is optional. False. Having a bank account can actually help you keep track of your finances. Most banks give you the option of keeping track of your account online. You need two accounts: a checking account and a savings account.

worth thinking about

▶ Using an Excel sheet to list every bill and all incoming finances will help you stay organized.

▶ You should never touch your savings account. If you put 5 percent to 10 percent of each paycheck in your savings, you can accumulate a large lump sum in a short amount of time.

▶ Budgeting your money does not mean you cannot spend money on fun stuff. It just means you need to be smart about it. You should figure to save 5 percent of your monthly income on clothes or entertainment.

If you fail to plan, you plan to fail.
Author Unknown

14 question

How do you deal with credit cards and debt?

If you were a ship and life an ocean, then debt would represent flooding within the ship. Debt can detour or completely sink you if you are not careful. Debt can come in all sorts of forms, but credit cards are often the main culprit. The best way to deal with debt is simple: do not get in it. However, if you find yourself taking on water, here are some tips:

answer

Credit cards for credit. Credit cards themselves are not all bad. In fact, having one can help you establish credit. Get rid of cards with high credit limits. Choosing cards with low credit levels helps you avoid getting too far in debt.

Do not carry a balance. Never spend more money than you can pay off that month. Keep your balance at zero. This helps your credit score and prevents you from falling behind.

Low interest rates. Many credit cards have high interest rates. A good interest rate is between 7 percent and 18 percent. If a card has an interest rate over 20 percent, avoid that card. Some credit card interest rates fluctuate, so keep an eye on those.

Do not pay just the minimum balance. You do not want to find yourself in the trap of paying only the minimum amount due. This never allows you to get rid of what you owe, and it even adds to your amount, because each time you pay off the minimum amount the interest collects on your debt.

Do not owe friends. Credit cards are not the only problem. Do everything you can to avoid borrowing money from friends or family members. If you are not able to pay them back, this will affect something worse than your credit score. Relationships can go through tremendous hardships when money is involved.

Do not pay bills late. Do everything you can to pay your bills on time. If you do not, you end up wasting your hard-earned cash on late fees. After a while, this can take a large chunk out of your checking account.

worth thinking about

▶ **When first starting** out, it can be difficult to establish credit. One idea is to apply first for a department store card. Be cautious, and do not overspend.

▶ **Avoid having more** than two or three cards. There is no need to have many cards.

▶ **Two forms of debt** are more acceptable than other forms of debt. Buying a home and getting an education often require loans. These investments, however, should bring in money in the future.

> *The rich rule over the poor, and the borrower is a slave to the lender.*
> Proverbs 22:7, HCSB

question

How can you save money?

Was there that one person in your school who never seemed to be part of the in-crowd? Were his clothes never the newest fashions? Was his car beat-up and rusty? If you knew this person (especially if you made fun of him), you may want to find him and apologize to him because there are a few things you can learn from him. Saving money may not be glamorous, but it pays off in the end.

answer

As you launch your adult life, you should adopt the principle of delayed gratification. It is easy in today's cultural climate to want everything now, but living outside your means leads to issues down the road. Deal with this now. Live with less when others don't so that later you might be able to live with more when others can't. The following are some tips on how to do that:

Buy used cars. Cars lose their value the moment you drive them off the lot, so it is better to buy a used one because they are cheaper. Do not get into a situation where you are paying monthly installments on a vehicle when you can barely make payments on your other bills. Nickname your car Lazarus, because you should keep fixing it every time it dies.

Cut excess bills. You should look at your bills to determine if you can eliminate any or, at the very least, minimize any. Having cable is not a necessity. Having a landline and a cell phone is extremely wasteful if you do not need both. Using less air-conditioning in the summer and less heat in the winter can reduce power bills.

Rent movies. If you need entertainment from time to time, renting movies is far cheaper than seeing them in the theater.

Join with friends. To save even more money, carpool with your friends to cut down on gas consumption. Also, rotate making dinner with your friends. Splitting costs can reduce food expenses.

worth thinking about

▶ Eating out can be demanding on your budget, so reduce the number of times you go to restaurants.

▶ Be a coupon scout. It may take a little bit of time, but you can save money by looking for special deals in the newspaper.

▶ Shop for clothes at discount stores. You can get name-brand clothes at thrift stores and places like Value City, Ross, and Marshall's.

> *Being frugal does not mean being cheap! It means being economical and avoiding waste.*
> Catherine Pulsifer

16

How do you schedule your time?

While you were in school, much of your schedule was planned for you. You woke up in time to get to class, and the rest of your day was set in stone. Class bell rings, class starts. Class bell rings again, class ends. When classes were over for the day, you were off to do homework or an extracurricular activity like a sport or a special club. Now that you have graduated, you have to set your own schedule.

answer

Obligations and business do not have a cutoff time as your classes did. Therefore, here are some tips on how to schedule your time:

Set time aside. Once a week, set time aside to go over all your appointments, projects, and events. This is a good time to go to a coffee shop or visit the beach. Review all your responsibilities and contrast them with the amount of time you have. Even if you do not like routine, a simple one such as this helps give you balance.

Keep a calendar. Keep a master calendar that has everything in it. Be sure to write in deadlines and meeting times as soon as they come up so that you do not forget. You can even keep your calendar on your phone or computer.

Say no. Learn to say no if you tend to overbook yourself. You cannot do anything well if you spread yourself thin.

Do one fun thing. Make sure to schedule something you enjoy no matter how busy you get. It may be running, reading, or hanging out with friends. Hard work is admirable, but all work and no play is for the birds—the cuckoo birds!

Plan rest. Rest is not the same as play. Running a marathon may be fun to you, but it is not rest. You need to relax. If you have to schedule relaxation to make it happen, do it. Take at least one day off a week. Every six months, be sure to take off a weekend. Every year, plan for a two-week vacation.

worth thinking about

▶ **Never get so busy** that you cannot maintain healthy relationships. You know you are too busy if you cannot connect with those you love.

▶ **Be sure not** to overlook scheduling conflicts. Having a monthly and a weekly calendar may help. New electronic devices even have alarms that go off to remind you of important dates and times.

▶ **Scheduling may seem** like a waste of time, but if you do it right it can help give you more time.

> *The plans of the diligent lead to profit*
> *as surely as haste leads to poverty.*
> Proverbs 21:5, NIV

What is true love?

Love is not love
Which alters when it alteration finds,
Or bends with the remover to remove:
O, no! it is an ever-fixed mark,
That looks on tempests and is never shaken;
It is the star to every wandering bark,
Whose worth's unknown,
although his height be taken.

William Shakespeare

17

question

What does a good résumé look like?

You have spent the last few years of your life preparing for the outside world. Many sleepless nights were full of homework and sweat in order for you to get that diploma. You never had to worry about what the words would be on that diploma. You just had to work hard. However, now you must come up with a résumé that allows you to get a job so you can work.

answer

Somehow, this little piece of paper is supposed to tell everyone that you are prepared for the next phase of life. This is why it is important to know how to prepare a good résumé. Here are some tips:

Content. Always tell the truth. If you lie, it often comes back to haunt you. Be specific by targeting one field. Do not use one résumé for several different fields.

Tone. You want to highlight your strengths. Do not draw attention to your weaknesses. Be positive and upbeat. Avoid listing things that might prevent an employer from hiring you.

Format. A bullet format makes your résumé easier to read. Typically, résumés should be no longer than one page. Do not use a font smaller than ten point or larger than twelve, and use a basic font style such as Times New Roman. You may want to see if the company you are applying to has guidelines with regard to its applications. If so, then conform your résumé to the company's specifications.

Layout. One popular way to lay out your résumé is in chronological order. This is especially helpful if most of your work experience is in the same field. Another way is to group work experiences according to subject matter. This is helpful when a person has experience in several different capacities.

Common mistakes. Do not forget to state your job objective. State what you want to do. Also, do not put so much in your résumé that there is no white space. Quality is always better than quantity.

worth thinking about

▶ Clarify your gender if your name could be male or female. If your name is Pat, for instance, be sure to use Mr., Ms., Miss, or Mrs.

▶ If you do not have a lot of work experience, then do relevant volunteer work. Also, do not forget to list odd jobs. If you mow lawns during the summer, for instance, you can put down Lawn Care (Self-Employed).

▶ Proofread your résumés. Do all you can to keep from embarrassing yourself with a simple but awkward typo.

> *Accomplishments: Completed thirteen years of high school.*
> Unwise Résumé Sample

question

How do you practice what you know?

After studying for the last several years, you should have all sorts of information rolling around in your brain. With the tests you took, the papers you wrote, and the presentations you gave, some of that knowledge had to have stuck. The real question is if you know how to use what you know in a practical manner. Playing baseball on the Xbox does not mean you are able to join Major League Baseball.

answer

You may have already come to this conclusion on your own, but you simply do not know how to use what you know. However, if you do not realize it, experience is what most employers are looking for. If you want to get a job in management, you need to have been a leader in something more than the winning side of the great water-balloon fight back in elementary school.

Even if you plan to continue your education, you need to be involved in the areas you plan to go into later on in life as a career. For instance, if you want to be a pastor one day, you need to get involved in ministry ASAP. If you were hiring, would you pick someone who has a degree but no experience or someone who has been in ministry successfully for a couple of years?

The first thing you should do is to find a place to practice what you know. If you want to become a personal trainer, you need to find a gym where you can be active. The second thing you should do is to find someone who knows more about your selected field than you do. Pick that person's brain about all he or she knows. Even if you have to pick up the tab for coffee, learn what you need and get the landscape of the field that interests you. Last, start doing. Most knowledge comes through trial and error, so do not try to understand everything before you start.

worth thinking about

▶ Start hanging around people who have similar goals as you. You can often learn a lot just by watching others in what they do.

▶ Keep practicing what you do even if you decide to further your education. When you stop, it is easy to get rusty.

▶ The first step is often the most difficult. Do not worry so much about anything other than the next step in front of you.

> *For every pass I caught in a game,*
> *I caught a thousand in practice.*
> Don Hutson

question

How do you survive cooking on your own?

Brace yourself! You are about to hear earth-shattering news that may devastate you beyond imagination. You cannot live off Burger King, Taco Bell, and Chick-fil-A the rest of your life! As tough as that might be, you have to move on and learn the basics of cooking on your own. You will manage, because you will learn how to survive. Moreover, Pizza Hut is not the answer.

answer

To be able to survive cooking on your own, you are going to need to make a friend. Her name is Erica, E-R-I-C-A. She will get you started on how to cook:

Eat simple. You should eat every meal of the day. This does not mean that you need to whip up a gourmet dish three times a day, but you do need to eat three meals a day. For instance, you can boil eggs the night before so that if you need to run out the door in the morning you can grab one or two before heading out.

Refrigerate your food. Your food will spoil much faster if you leave it at room temperature. You can put grains like bread and cereal in the refrigerator to keep them fresher longer.

Invite guests. Some people do better at cooking certain types of food. Others just get more motivated to cook when they have people to cook for. Either way, invite people over so you can cook for them. Perhaps they can contribute one of their specialty dishes.

Cook for days. Rather than cooking one meal at a time, cook a large amount of a recipe and eat on it for the next couple of days. Some foods are often better the second time around.

Add appliances. Having appliances like a microwave oven, a countertop grill, and a sandwich maker can go a long way. Microwave ovens cook faster. Small grills are great for chicken breasts and hamburgers. Sandwich makers allow you to be a bit creative with unusual but tasty ingredients in addition to the basic grilled cheese.

worth thinking about

▶ **If you find** a sale or you just buy a lot of your food at one time, using the freezer for bread and meat can help keep them fresh.

▶ **With a sandwich maker,** provolone cheese, pepperoni, and a bit of marinara sauce can instantly produce a mini pizza pocket. Sandwich makers are good for desserts and French toast, too.

▶ **Try not to live** off ramen noodles, but if you do have them, add meat and veggies for a fuller meal.

> *A hungry stomach seldom scorns plain food.*
> Horace

question
▼
How do you clean your home?

Not everyone can afford to hire workers to clean up their messes. Although having a cleaning service may sound appealing, it is not realistic for the average graduate. There is no getting around the fact that you will clutter and dirty things up, however. You need to know how to pick up after yourself. You will want to invite others to your place, and you will need a good environment in which to relax.

answer
▼
Make your life easier and get an organizer bucket that has a handle on it so you have all your cleaniing supplies in one container that is easily transportable. You will need these essentials: an all-purpose cleaner in a spray bottle (for glass and surface), paper towels or rags, a toothbrush (use your old one), a duster (not a feather duster—it just makes the dust fly around), all-purpose wipes (for a quick cleanup), powdered cleaner (better to use one without bleach since bleach isn't good to breathe in), disposable toilet bowl pads, shower spray, and rubber gloves.

To keep your place clean, you need to keep up with it consistently. Plan to appoint one day a week to clean. If you do a little bit at a time, you save yourself from cleaning a major mess later. If you have roommates, you can share the load by alternating chores with them.

Keep up as much as possible with cleaning toilets, tubs, sinks, and shared areas like the kitchen or the living room. Be sure to vacuum before you dust, because some vacuum cleaners spread dust back into the air. When cleaning the kitchen, avoid using sponges because they hold bacteria more than cloths, which you wash more frequently. Use separate cloths for dishes and for counters. When you clean the bathroom, use an all-purpose cleaner. Be sure to clean the entire toilet. Save the floors for last. Sweep the floor first and then mop it.

worth thinking about

▶ Try to stay away from cleaners that contain bleach or caustic ingredients that are harmful to breathe in.

▶ Some brands such as Holy Cow not only clean nearly everything in your home but also are environmentally friendly.

▶ If you are low on money, use vinegar. Vinegar is excellent for cleaning floors, counters, bathrooms, and just about everything. Undiluted vinegar in a spray bottle will clean mirrors and windows—wipe dry with newspaper.

> *Cleanliness is, indeed, next to godliness.*
> John Wesley

question

What kind of place should you live in?

Choosing where you live is one of the biggest decisions you will make because the place you live affects various aspects of your life. Remember when another girl's locker was next to the locker of the boy you liked? It gave her the chance to talk to him nearly every day while yours was fifteen lockers down. How about when the class dance was in the gym and it was hard to enjoy because the place smelled like sweaty feet? Location and environment influence your experience.

answer

There are several options you need to consider when deciding where you should live:

With parents. Living with parents is a plus for some and a minus to others. It depends on your circumstances. If you are just finishing high school and are trying to save money while going to school, this is fine. However, if you are just finishing college or are planning to go directly into the workforce, you need to have a six-month goal to get out on your own. You need to start paying your own way.

Dorm. If you plan to further your education, living on campus is always an option. In dorm situations, you can meet new people and get into the social scene a bit faster. Dorm living can be cheaper than living on your own, and often you do not have to buy your own furniture. Some schools even have on-campus apartments that offer some privacy without all of the craziness that can be associated with dorm life.

Buying vs. renting. If you have the resources to buy a home and plan on being there for a few years, this is a much smarter move, because you can sell it or rent it out once you move. If you get roommates, your payment per month can be about the same as renting.

Convenience vs. glamour. Choose convenience over glamour in the beginning. If you can live closer to your job or the campus, do so instead of getting the nice beachfront home.

worth thinking about

▶ With regard to living with parents, the only two exceptions are if you experience extreme financial hardships or if a loved one is sick and needs care.

▶ Before you live in a dorm, you will want to check out the environment. Many are coed, and even more are extremely rowdy and difficult to live in for a variety of reasons.

▶ Be sure to pick a place where you feel safe. Do your research before committing to an area.

> *My people will live in a peaceful habitation, and in secure dwellings and in undisturbed resting places.*
> Isaiah 32:18, NAS

question

Should you get a roommate?

For some people, the thought of getting a roommate is exciting because a roomie offers social interaction and someone to hang out with. For others this is exactly why they do not want a roommate. When moving out on your own, you must cross this bridge. Perhaps you like to try new things, or perhaps you do not. Either way, there are both advantages and disadvantages to having roommates. Here are a few:

answer

Disadvantages

1. Having a roommate can be frustrating if you like things a particular way. If you are clean, it might be tough if your roommate does not share your same sense of upkeep.

2. Some people may be more confrontational than you are, and you may have to deal with a clash of personalities and expectations in your interpersonal interactions.

3. Having a roommate can take up personal time. If you prefer quiet, your roommate may like to have a bit more interaction than you do.

Advantages

1. A roommate can be fun to hang out with and offer friendship. This is especially true if you plan on going to a new place. Some roommates offer to show you around and even connect you to possible social outlets.

2. Having a roommate can help defer costs. Living alone can start to add up after a while, so splitting your bills with another person can be a wise move.

3. Having a roommate can stretch you. Everyone has his or her likes and dislikes, and if you live alone you can become entrenched in your way. Having a roommate can help you in that you have to get used to living and negotiating with another human being.

worth thinking about

▶ **It would be smart** to screen a potential roommate before you make the final decision to be roomies. Getting references is not abnormal.

▶ **Because everyone** lives differently, set up a system for cleaning and for paying bills. Consult everyone's opinion so that it is not only one person dictating the rules.

▶ **If an issue arises,** take care of it right away. Do not let it fester. If you do, it could build up and explode in a way you might regret later.

> *Better a dry crust with peace and quiet*
> *than a house full of feasting, with strife.*
> Proverbs 17:1, NIV

question

How do you act at your new job?

Entering a new job can be intimidating. Those dreams you had where you were in front of the entire class in just your underwear are not unlike going into your new job. It is easy to feel exposed and embarrassed. It is as though everyone else can see your glaring flaws. When you feel exposed, it is easy to feel small. The fact that you may not know what to expect compounds your feelings of exposure and embarrassment.

answer

Here are some tips on what you should do in your new job. All you need to do is know your vowels. They are A, E, I, O, U, and sometimes Y (Why):

Address needs. When starting a new job, pay attention to the needs of the company. See what is not being done, and when you have the chance address those needs.

Extra mile. If you are asked to get something done, do not be satisfied doing only what you have to do to get by—do more. If your boss wants the report in two days, do everything you can to get it done in one. If your boss asks you to put together a sales presentation, make sure you put extra details and research into it.

Initiate with others. It is easy when you are new to wait for others to approach you, but some people are even more afraid of meeting you, are shy themselves, or are so busy they do not think to introduce themselves.

On time. Be sure to be on time to everything. The last thing you want to do is give the wrong impression by showing up late to your job.

Understand culture. Every organization has a different culture. Some cultures are formal; some are informal. Whichever yours is, follow the protocols and adjust your interactions.

Y (why): Do not be afraid to ask questions. Your new employer will not expect you to know everything right away.

worth thinking about

▶ Asking questions may show that you are interested in learning. Some employers like to share company knowledge.

▶ Some employers may interpret showing up late as a sign of disrespect. It often says, "I'm more important than you, so I will show up when I want."

▶ If you do decide to address a need, be sure not to do someone else's job. You do not want to step on someone's toes. Ask permission first.

> *Work hard and become a leader;*
> *be lazy and become a slave.*
> Proverbs 12:24, NLT

question

▼

How should you not act at your new job?

Sometimes the most difficult things to know are what not to do. It is a good guess that you wished you knew not to lick frozen metal poles before that incident in the third grade. You live and learn, but sometimes you wish you had learned a little sooner. As you start your new job and begin the next phase of your life, you should know that there are major things you should avoid doing.

answer

▼

No company is perfect, so you will be tempted to get involved in all sorts of situations. Here are some you want to stay away from:

Gossip. Nothing can be more dangerous than engrossing yourself in the watercooler talk. Employees pass rumors in the workplace the way players pass footballs at a game. You want to keep your name out of the headlines as much as possible, and you start by not listening to or conveying gossip.

Brownnosing. Doing a good job is different from brown-nosing your supervisor. Brownnosing is a form of manipulation. An example of this would be telling your boss that he is head and shoulders above Donald Trump, when in reality he can't run a lemonade stand. Brownnosing is not a good way to get what you want.

Politics. There are often different camps in one company. If two people are up for a promotion, people often take sides and use power plays to get results. Do not get caught up in the games—they can end up biting you in the end.

Slack. After a while, many people figure out the minimum work they need to put forth to keep from being fired. Always try to give your best even if others do not.

Devolve. Even good organizations can have environments that go against your personal value system. Do not be lulled into being more like the organization's sense of right and wrong rather than your own sense of right and wrong.

worth thinking about

▶ **Brownnosing often** irks fellow workers and even employers.

▶ **Some companies** have such a competitive climate that people do anything to get their way. Before you know it, you may become someone you do not even like.

▶ **If you choose** a side in a political battle at work, you risk being on the losing side. If the new boss knows you didn't want him or her, your job security may fade.

> *Never slander a worker to the employer, or the person will curse you, and you will pay for it.*
> Proverbs 30:10, NLT

question

How important are people skills?

You may have been the class clown or the class president, but this does not mean you have good people skills. Now that you have graduated, you will need to reach beyond mere charisma and truly learn how to interact with people. To learn people skills you must first know what they are. People skills are important because they are the skills that help you interact with other people. To do your best work, you must master people skills.

answer

Hard skills. Hard skills are technical or administrative elements of an organization's core business. These may or may not include machine protocols, computer procedures, safety standards, financial plans, and sales administration. These are generally easy to observe and measure quantifiably. Hard skills are typically brand-new information, so unlearning is not always needed.

Soft skills. Soft skills, known as "people skills," are harder to quantify and measure. These skills include communicating, problem solving, conflict resolution, listening, dialogue, and team dynamics, to name a few. Soft skills not only are harder to measure, but they can also be harder to teach since every person has learned by experience how to relate to people. If one has learned to relate to others in an unhealthy way, then unlearning must occur. For example, if your family resolves conflicts through raised voices and hot tempers, you should unlearn these behaviors.

Do you remember the scene at the spring dance at school? A semipopular boy walked up to a pretty girl and whispered something to her. Her smile became anger as she slapped him across the cheek. She stormed off, leaving the boy standing in bewilderment. This is an example of saying the wrong thing at the wrong time. You do not want this scene to be you and a coworker. If you master soft skills, you can improve your job performance.

worth thinking about

▶ **Some leaders** may overlook the importance of soft skills. However, soft skills are actually more important than most of the hard skills.

▶ **The best way** to unlearn bad people skills is by applying and practicing good ones.

▶ **If you do not** know how well you are doing in the area of people skills, ask people you trust, such as your family, teachers, and friends.

> *Attention to these softer skills will reduce turnover, increase productivity, and generate more business for the firm.*
> Stephen E. Seckler

question

Are you able to network?

The excitement of graduation is in the rearview mirror, and the dawn of tomorrow is straight ahead. A new job or even a new school to further one's education can be daunting. New faces and new places can be overwhelming if you do not know what to do. If you are to succeed in the real world, you need to know how to meet and network with people.

answer

It wasn't that long ago that you had to enter the lunchroom not knowing where to sit but hoping you wouldn't have to sit all alone. As you continue in life, you will learn that you will not be able to do everything on your own. You will need to network—to multiply your own resources by connecting with others and combining your resources. Following are the 7 C's to networking:

Contact. Some people simply do not know how to begin. One idea is simply to say hello and introduce yourself. Another approach is to ask the other person a question: "Aren't you the senior adviser for KINN Electronics?"

Common ground. Once you make contact, find a topic of mutual interest: "Cool. I actually interned at KINN last year."

Concentrate. Make eye contact and respond to what the person says to show that you are interested. It is vital to focus on the person you are speaking to and not on yourself.

Consider needs. Be aware of the other person's needs, especially if you might be an answer to them.

Convey your thoughts. Offer your assistance or convey positive feedback to meet those needs: "I'm quite familiar with that software. If you'd like, I could assist you."

Contact info. If the conversation is productive, offer your card or contact information. Oftentimes the person will give you a business card without asking. If not, politely ask for it.

Consistent. Keep the connection active. Follow up by sending an e-mail or making a phone call.

worth thinking about

▶ **When connecting with** others, honestly keep their best interests at heart. Some folks are great at networking, but they have only their own interests in mind. Remember that no one wants to be treated like a slot machine. Do not invest in someone only to gain from him.

▶ **When exchanging** information, be sure to note which form of communication your contacts prefer. Many prefer e-mail to phone calls because it is less intrusive, they can answer at their convenience, and it is faster.

▶ **Always follow up.** Do not chance losing a valuable connection through inattention or neglect.

> *The way of the world is meeting people through other people.*
> Robert Kerrigan

How should I interact with others?

To the weak I became weak, to win the weak. I have become all things to all men so that by all possible means I might save some.

1 Corinthians 9:22, NIV

question

▼

What are tools you can use to network?

A car with no engine goes nowhere. A car with no wheels not only isn't going anywhere, but it doesn't look very appealing, either. The same is true for your career. Without the right tools, you will stall on the professional highway. These tools are ways to exchange, convey, or promote information about who you are and what you do. When used correctly, these tools can add to your projected value to those with whom you are seeking to connect.

answer

▼

In this technically advanced generation, you can utilize multiple tools to aid you in networking. There are a few necessities, however. The basic tools include:

Business card. Everyone should have a business card. Not only should you have one, but you should also have one that stands out from other cards. Some cards are transparent, some are a slightly different size, and some have your picture on it. Your card should include your full name and contact information: phone number, e-mail address, and in some cases your mailing address.

Social networking sites. MySpace, Facebook, Bebo, and similar sites are becoming so popular that even companies have their own. MySpace and Facebook seem to be the most used and most effective. Using social sites for networking means that your page should be professional and uncontroversial. You can use the blog sections on MySpace for your résumé.

Personal Web site. A Web site should follow the preceding suggestions. A Web site is an excellent tool for networking if you choose not to network on a social site.

E-mail. E-mail is necessary in today's world. Gmail, AOL, Yahoo, and Hotmail are all good places to get an e-mail account. When choosing a screen name, choose something professional or catchy.

Cell phone. Cell phones are better than landlines because you can use them anywhere.

worth thinking about

▶ **When using** social networking sites, you may want to use the privacy settings so that only people you select can view your page.

▶ **While using** a cell phone, be careful when texting people of the opposite sex. Many people who are married (and even some who aren't) see this as inappropriate communication.

▶ **You should always** have a business card with you. Keep it in your wallet or purse, because you never know when you may need it.

> *Doing business without advertising is like winking at a girl in the dark. You know what you are doing, but nobody else does.*
> Stuart Henderson

question

Do you listen?

Have you been called upon in the middle of class to answer a question, only to realize that you have no idea what the question was? If so, you know how helpless and embarrassing it can be. It is one thing to not know the answer to the question, but it is another to have no idea what the question was. How mortifying. The importance of listening grows as you face your postgraduation life.

answer

Being able to hear someone is not listening. It is possible to hear every syllable and yet miss entirely what the other person is saying to you. If you truly want to listen, do the following:

Be other-focused. Focus on the person you are speaking to. It is easy to listen to others through self-focused ears. Instead of wondering how what is said affects you, try empathizing with the speaker. This includes paying attention to things you might not care about. Center the conversation on the speaker's thoughts and feelings.

Avoid judging. Without judging, listen to what the person is saying. Be supportive rather than attempt to fix the problems that you perceive.

Avoid assuming. Do not read too much into situations . If no one said it, do not reach too much. Reaching too much can lead to major issues. If Tim says he is just tired, don't think that he is having marital issues. Instead, ask clarifying questions to make sure you really are hearing what the other person is saying.

Use positive communicators. As Erica talks to you, be sure to nod your head to let her know you are hearing her. Small words like *really, uh-huh,* and *okay* show that you are active in the conversation and at the same time still allow Erica to be the center of the conversation. If you say nothing and show no emotion, you may come across as if you have tuned out or are disapproving.

worth thinking about

▶ **When asking** questions, ask open questions. These types of questions allow the other person to respond with more than a yes or no. "Can you think of a time when you were happy?" instead of "Are you happy?"

▶ **If you do not** know if the person wants advice or simply wants you to listen, ask what he or she wants from you.

▶ **Do not say,** "I know how you feel." Most times you do not know how the other person feels, and it can be upsetting if you pretend that you do.

> *Anyone who has ears should listen!*
> Matthew 11:15, HCSB

29

Why is eye contact important?

The eyes are the window to the soul. You see others through your eyes, and others see you by looking into your eyes. Even though many organizations are professional and sometimes not overly personal, it is important to understand the role eye contact plays in your one-on-one interactions. Consider what messages your eye contact might relay, and recognize that what you think others are communicating may not be what they mean.

answer

The importance of eye contact is likely not a foreign concept to you. When that special someone looks into your eyes, you know what your loved one is thinking. If someone avoids eye contact, this clues you into the other person's thoughts. Culture and gender affect how a person uses eye contact.

Culture. Typically, in America, making eye contact is a sign of respect. It also indicates that one person is paying attention to the other person. In some cultures, *not* making eye contact is a sign of respect. In many Asian cultures and even in some African-American families, this is the case. Try to keep cultural considerations in mind when you interpret another's actions.

Gender. Women tend to like eye contact, especially if they are talking to you. Men tend to process as they listen and sometimes do not consider eye contact as important.

Avoiding good eye contact can be viewed as:

Insecure. It is not a good thing for someone to view you as insecure if you hope to be in a leadership position. An employer may interpret lack of eye contact as an inability to make tough decisions.

Deceptive. Some people may think if you cannot make eye contact you have something to hide.

Not interested. Other people may think that you just do not care what they say.

worth thinking about

▶ **Do not stare** too long or people might think you are odd or even think you are dangerous. Staring too long makes others uncomfortable.

▶ **Try not to stare** at people too much when you are not talking to them. If you are caught looking, people may think you are checking them out.

▶ **If you are** interacting with someone of another culture or background, keep in mind that another's social interactions may have different protocols.

> *Men are born with two eyes, but only one tongue, in order that they should see twice as much as they say.*
> Charles Caleb Colton

question

What does a handshake say about you?

There are many forms of greeting others throughout the world. How you greet someone depends largely on the culture and relationship. In some parts of the world, you bow to each other as a greeting. In others, you kiss on the cheek once, twice, and in some places even three times! In Bible times, people greeted each other with a brotherly kiss, too. In the professional world, however, a handshake is the appropriate greeting.

answer

Your handshake can say a lot about you. If you are unaware, your handshake may even convey something you would prefer it didn't. Get yourself started on the right track by being cautious of the following hand-shakes:

Too hard. If you try to squeeze off the hand of the person you are meeting, the person will likely see you as some-one who is trying to prove something. Confidence is one thing, but squeezing can come across more as mean. At the very least, it may come across as inconsiderate. If the person is not as strong as you are, a too-hard handshake can be a turnoff. This should not be surprising—not too many people like their hand crushed.

Too weak. You also do not want to be too weak with your handshake. Having a firm grip is a good thing. If your handshake is as limp as an unconscious fish, others will likely see you as insecure and scared. Let others know you are there by having a reasonable grip. Use the same firmness you would use to open a door.

Power play. A power-play handshake twists both people's hands to where the power player ends up on top and the submissive hand goes underneath. People who tend to do this often like to make sure they are in control. Do not do this. You will intimidate some by it, and you will turn off others who are also strong personalities. Besides, it is just odd to twist someone's hand while shaking it.

worth thinking about

▶ **Do not keep** the grip of the handshake too long. Two firm shakes are quite enough.

▶ **When you wear** a nametag, be sure to put it on your right. This way when you shake with your right hand it puts your name in the other person's line of sight.

▶ **Make sure your** hands are dry. Do not make anyone guess why your palms are wet. At meetings, hand sanitizer may be a better option than water.

> *If you greet only your brothers, what more are you doing than others? Do not even the Gentiles do the same?*
> Matthew 5:47, NAS

question

Do you know how to read a room?

While you were in school, most of your classrooms likely had several chairs facing the front of the class so that everyone could clearly see the teacher. Your classroom had the purpose of holding a class, and the setup facilitated this function. Many rooms in business, like offices, conference rooms, and auditoriums, also have setups that communicate the purpose of the venue. When you enter a room, notice the setup so you can interpret the culture of the room.

answer

Long-tabled rooms. Oftentimes the setup of the room also indicates the personality and purpose of those within it. You are aware of personal space. You let only people you trust get close to you physically. In the business world, space also plays a major role. For example, if you are in a meeting and Mr. Jones chooses to be at the head of the table, he likely wants others to listen to him. By being at the end, everyone must look in the same direction to see him. However, if he decides to sit in the middle, then his main goal is likely to connect with others. By sitting in the middle, he places himself in the nearest proximity to the most people.

Office. There are three main office layouts. By putting the desk in the corner so that it is guarded by three barriers (two walls and desk), the occupant has formed a throne situation. This setup gives the most control and is the most uncomfortable for those sitting on the other side of the desk. Another office layout allows space in front of the desk and to the side. This is less threatening for the person sitting on the other side. The best setup for connecting is to have two separate seats apart from the desk. By sitting with you away from the desk, the person creates the optimal environment for connecting because the desk isn't there to create a barrier. By being aware of these room layouts, you can better interpret the expectations of those with whom you are speaking.

worth thinking about

▶ In a social setting, observe how close others are to each other. You can get a better idea about who feels more comfortable with whom by seeing how close they are when they speak.

▶ Notice what each person's personal space is. Do not exceed any person's comfort level.

▶ When you observe, be sure to realize that you will not always be right. Observing is usually not 100 percent accurate, but it can help.

> *Our sense of proxemics . . . [is] culture-bound, internalized by us as the result of the cultures we grew up in.*
>
> Lee Su Kim

question

▼

What does your body posture say?

Many people think of communication merely as words people speak in a particular conversation. However, much of what people communicate comes from expressions and posture. The word for communicating without speaking is *nonverbal*. If you frown, this nonverbal indicates you are unhappy without your ever having to say a word. Your body posture is a major nonverbal that communicates to those who see you.

answer

▼

Be aware that your nonverbals are more believable than what you say. If you tell someone that you love him or her but say it with a scowl, that person will likely find it difficult to believe you. If you know what body posture may say, then you can be intentional when you interact with people. Here are some key insights:

Folded arms. Crossing your arms can come across as though you are closing off and guarding yourself. It seems as though you are unapproachable. It may communicate that you are uncomfortable and are trying to protect yourself. It may also communicate that you are not open to whatever is being said.

Hands on hips. This one often reminds people of their mothers when they were being disciplined. This stance can make it appear that you are being overly authoritative. If this body posture coincides with constructive feedback, it may make your message too strong.

Slouching. Slouching communicates insecurity or laziness. Neither is the most positive thing to communicate. Be sure to stand up straight, keep your chin up, and put your shoulders back. By doing this you will look more confident and avoid looking like a slacker.

Clenched fists. Some people clench their fists when they are thinking and walking, or even when they are cold. Yet, clenched fists can come across as anger. When making gestures, keep your hands open.

worth thinking about

▶ While staying conscious of your body posture, make sure you have the right expression on your face. When meeting someone, smile. When you hear someone yelling at someone else in the office, do not smile.

▶ If you notice that your posture may say something you do not want, it is okay to mention it. Tell whomever you are talking to that you are crossing your arms because you are cold and not because you are upset.

▶ Stand in front of the mirror to see how you look to others.

> *The language of the body is the key that can unlock the soul.*
> Konstantin Stanislavsky

question

What is mirroring?

Some women and men spend countless hours in front of the mirror. Sometimes people spend hours admiring what reflects back at them, and sometimes they lament what they see. Brushes, makeup, hair products, and that perfect outfit combine to portray the best possible look for you. This is not mirroring. Mirroring is something you do more for the other than for yourself, and you need to know how to do it in order to succeed.

answer

Mirroring has nothing to do with the reflective glass on your wall. It has more to do with your observation skills. Mirroring keeps you plugged into the conversation. It is an action, which means you have to act. Mirroring is watching the person you are talking to and mimicking what he or she does. This does not mean that you repeat exactly what the other person says until he gets irritated at you. That is what your little brother used to do when you were kids.

People like to connect with people who are like themselves. There is something challenging about connecting with someone different from you. The bigger the differences between the two of you, the greater the challenge.

So do your best to match the other person. Here are some examples of mirroring:

Volume. When you are talking to someone, notice his or her speaking volume. If Stephanie is a soft-spoken person, speak gently. If you talk too loud, she may get overwhelmed. If Rick is a loud talker, speak up a bit. Matching what a person does can help him open up and feel more comfortable with you.

Body language. If Jason is leaning forward, you should lean in a bit as well. If he is trying to tell you something, your leaning shows him you are interested. If Josh leans back with his arms crossed, then do the same. Leaning into Josh when he leans back might come across to him as invading his personal space. Crossing arms and legs along with the person you are talking to can help the person feel more at ease.

worth thinking about

▶ Match the other person's expressions. If he is upset, do not smile. If he is happy, do not frown or act aloof.

▶ Do not be obvious about your mirroring. Do it in very subtle ways. The last thing you want is for him to think you are copying him. Do not change your position the moment he does. Wait a beat or two.

▶ Take time to observe people and the difference in the ways they interact with one another.

> To the weak I became weak, in order to win the weak. I have become all things to all people, so that I may by all means save some.
> 1 Corinthians 9:22, HCSB

question

How do you handle conflict?

Some people do everything they can to avoid conflict. Others thrive on drama. However, neither of these approaches will work if you hope to be successful after graduation. The truth is, no matter how hard you try, you will eventually find yourself in a situation where conflict is inevitable. Conflict itself is not always a bad thing if you handle it correctly. Do you know how to handle conflict?

answer

There are ways to handle conflict that leave all parties involved feeling better about themselves when it is over. The following are suggestions to help you handle conflict in the best way possible:

Use facts. When in a conflict situation, it is always better to stick with facts than to fling emotions. Rather than telling Paul you were hacked off that he swooped in and stole your commission, simply point out that you were the first to establish contact with the customer and that the commission, therefore, should go to you.

Be honest. Do not hide or stretch the truth. As you live an honest life, people will take your word over the word of others who are less than forthright.

Do not question intentions. Be sure to focus on actions and not intentions. Even if you suspect someone of wrong-doing, you do not know his true intentions. Questioning intentions will immediately put your coworker on the defensive. Instead of saying, "I know you meant to hurt my feelings," simply say, "I'm not sure if you intended to hurt me, but I was hurt."

Use "I" statements. Instead of saying *you* did this and *you* did that, try using "I" statements. Saying things like "*You* are so frustrating when *you* try to bully me" can come off as attacking. However, if you say, "*I* get frustrated when *I* feel as though *I* am being bullied," it shows that you are merely sharing how you feel and not blaming the other person. Saying *you* a lot comes across more as an accusation.

worth thinking about

▶ **Pick your timing** wisely when you confront people. If you take issue with everything, people will eventually tune you out. Do your best not to always expect the worst of people. Assume the best intentions.

▶ **Once you have** handled a situation, let it go. Do not stew on any one conflict too long.

▶ **No matter how** upset or vocal someone else gets, do all you can to stay calm. By staying calm, you keep a stronger sense of clarity in the situation.

> *If your brother sins against you, go and show him his fault, just between the two of you.*
> Matthew 18:15, NIV

question

▼

How do you improve your e-mail etiquette?

Knowing how to send e-mails is necessary in today's professional landscape. Many employers prefer to communicate via e-mail at first because it is quicker and less intrusive. It may seem far less personal to you, but even if it is you must learn how to navigate this medium professionally to avoid sending the wrong message, even if unintentional. Now is a good time to ask yourself if you know how to improve your e-mail etiquette.

answer

▼

You should start by making sure that you have a professional and friendly e-mail name. You do not want your e-mail handle to make you look unprofessional or worse. Names like: biker88@e-mail.com and downwith-treehuggers@e-mail.com have to go. Select a combination of your name or specific field to be safe.

If you have not yet established a relationship with the individual you are e-mailing, it is important to use a title (e.g., Dr., Mr., or Ms.). When e-mailing a female, be safe and use Ms. rather than Mrs. or Miss. Do not assume familiarity until you have established a relationship with the individual. If after a few e-mails you are unsure how to address the person, it is okay to ask.

If you do not get a response right away, be sure to wait at least one to two weeks before e-mailing again. He or she is likely busy, and you want to avoid bombarding the individual further.

Be sensitive to using all CAPS in an e-mail, because all caps are interpreted as yelling at the person who ends up reading it.

Utilize the subject box in your e-mail so that the person receiving the e-mail knows what the e-mail is about. If it is in response to a job opening, refer to the job title as the subject, such as Open Sales Position.

Ask permission before attaching files. There are many viruses out there, so some companies have protocols on when and how they accept attachments.

worth thinking about

▶ Use the subject box to notify the recipient who you are and the purpose of the e-mail. If the person already knows you, you can type your name in the subject box.

▶ In formal e-mails, steer clear of using too many ellipses (. . .) or all lowercase letters in an e-mail.

▶ It is also smart to include your contact info beneath your name at the end of an e-mail so that the recipient can contact you.

> *I get mail; therefore I am.*
> Scott Adams

question

▼

Can you give constructive feedback without offending?

Everyone likes to hear good feedback. Who doesn't want to know he did a good job? However, many people give feedback without regard to how the receiver may feel about it. Bluntness can crush the spirit of the other person. There is, however, a right way to give feedback to someone. You can actually be responsible for helping someone grow if you give feedback in the right way.

answer

▼

If someone is doing something wrong or simply could do something better, you may be the person who needs to talk to him. If you see an area of potential growth, do the following:

Act quickly. It is better to address something as soon as possible. The longer you wait to talk to an individual about something on your mind, the greater the chance you will boil over inside. The last thing you want is to explode at someone when you could have dealt with the situation more smoothly.

Approach the offender first. Have the decency to approach the person you have the issue with before you go to the boss. If you make an end run around other workers, you will likely get a bad name. No one likes being blind-sided. It comes off as a bit cowardly and self-serving to go to leadership prior to going to the person with whom you have the issue.

Use the sandwich method to offer feedback. First, set up your feedback by informing the individual that you have something to say. Second, offer a sincere compliment that is relevant. Third, give the evidence of the events that have occurred that led up to your desire to talk. Fourth, present how you felt and thought about what occurred. Fifth, offer a positive outlook so that the person has hope that this can be resolved. Last, follow up with this individual to make sure you are on the same page.

worth thinking about

▶ **Not every person** will respond well when confronted no matter how well you handle it. You are responsible for what you do, not what others do.

▶ **Give good feedback** from time to time. Do not be the person who points out only negatives. Some studies say that it takes seven positive comments to negate one negative comment.

▶ **Do not use** an opportunity to give feedback as a chance simply to get what you want. Stay away from trying to manipulate someone just to appease your desires.

> *He who listens to a life-giving rebuke*
> *will be at home among the wise.*
> Proverbs 15:31, NIV

What if God isn't meeting my expectations?

Oh, how great are God's riches and wisdom and knowledge! How impossible it is for us to understand his decisions and his ways! For who can know the Lord's thoughts? Who knows enough to give him advice? And who has given him so much that he needs to pay it back? For everything comes from him and exists by his power and is intended for his glory. All glory to him forever! Amen.

Romans 11:33–36, NLT

question

How do you accept criticism?

Even when someone means for criticism to be constructive, you can still feel put down. However, good feedback is not the same thing as an instructor trying to convince you that an *F* really stands for *fantastic*. Everyone has blind spots, so it is important that you listen to the people who take the time to invest in your personal development. The key to growing from negative feedback is knowing how to accept it.

answer

Following are eight *don'ts* for accepting feedback:

1. Don't take issue with something the speaker says, tune out, or think of a snappy response. This illustrates that you are defensive and not open to what the speaker has to say.

2. Don't repeatedly interrupt the speaker.

3. Don't say "Yeah, I know" a lot when people are speaking. This makes it look as though you are a know-it-all.

4. Don't space out while listening.

5. Don't believe you understand what is said until you seek confirmation. Believing you understand when you do not leads to misunderstandings.

6. Don't react with negative expressions, such as rolling your eyes.

7. Don't shift blame to others.

8. Don't make excuses.

Following are eight *do's* for accepting feedback:

1. Focus your attention on the speaker. This is not the time to slip into a daydream.

2. Be positive and intentional about nonverbals. Looking into the person's eyes and nodding your head indicate that you are listening.

3. Allow the speaker to finish before talking.

4. Interpret what is being said from that person's reference, framework, and feelings, not your own.

5. Restate what the person said to ensure understanding.

6. Ask questions to clarify what the person said.

7. Thank the individual for taking the time to talk to you, and say that you will consider it.

8. Take time to consider what areas you could improve upon.

worth thinking about

▶ **Being aware** of your body posture can benefit your awareness of nonverbal communication.

▶ **Constructive criticism** is feedback that could potentially help you grow in one area or another.

▶ **Note that verbal** abuse is different from constructive feedback. Verbal abuse holds no benefit to the listener.

> *An open rebuke is better than hidden love!*
> Proverbs 27:5, NLT

38 question

Why can't you have what you want when you want?

If you have ever heard the phrase "You can't have your cake and eat it too," you may wonder what that means. You may not even like cake. The point is that when you have one particular thing, it often prevents you from having something else. You may want the companionship of marriage. To be married you say good-bye to a bit of your independence. Part of life is accepting that you cannot have everything you want.

answer

It can be frustrating when you cannot have what you want when you want it. If there is something you desire, you need to know the following:

Ask. If you want something bad enough, the first thing you should do is ask God for it. Sometimes it is simply easier to sulk about what you do not have rather than to ask for it. The Bible says that you do not have because you do not ask. Try asking and see what happens.

Check motives. Why is it you want what you want? A person may want many things, and often those things are not good. Hitler wanted power, and you know that his motives were far from admirable. The Bible points out that you ask but do not have because you have wrong motives. There are times when you might want something that isn't the best thing for you or someone else. After a breakup, it might be easy to wish something negative on the other person simply because you are hurt and not because the other person deserves it.

Look at timing. Sometimes God waits for better timing to give you what you want. If you want to get married, God may ask you to wait until after you graduate or until you have a job. Sometimes silence is simply a "not yet."

Accepting no. Sometimes what you want may not be the right thing. Thankfully, God does not always give you what you ask for.

worth thinking about

▶ Trust that God has good things planned for you. Ask for what is in your heart, and wait patiently.

▶ Know that God is not a heavenly ATM. Seek first a relationship with Him. How would you feel if your friends were hanging out with you only because you give them stuff?

▶ Take some time to think back on things that you have asked for and that God has given to you. Think of the things you asked for but that for your own good God did not give you.

> *You ask and do not receive, because you ask with wrong motives, so that you may spend it on your pleasures.*
>
> James 4:3, NAS

question 39

What does *integrity* mean?

When you are younger, people expect you to bump your head a few times because you are learning. As you get older, however, people place more expectations on you. People expect a higher level of standards from you after your graduation. When you step over boundaries, you end up hurting more people than just yourself. This is why integrity is so important.

answer

God is far more concerned with how you do things than with what you do. If you own a multibillion-dollar company that gained its money through faulty ethics, God is not pleased. If you are a missionary to India but steal from the offering plate, God is not okay with that.

Integrity is doing the right thing the right way even when no one is looking. When you are alone and there are no witnesses, do you still do the right thing? What would you do if you saw a twenty-dollar bill drop from your coworker's wallet? Acting with integrity would mean handing back the twenty even if you could pocket it without anyone knowing.

Some people merely want to have the appearance of integrity. In fact, some people would rather *appear* to have integrity than actually *have* integrity. As an example of this, some innocent men are in prison while guilty parties still run high-profile companies.

True integrity is doing the right thing even if it hurts. Doing the right thing in some situations will cost you. If your boss asks you to do something you know is wrong, saying no might cost you your job. You might be out a paycheck, but in the end, you will come out on top. God rewards those who are faithful to doing the right thing the right way. Abraham, King David, and Joseph are good examples of this.

worth thinking about

▶ **Being humble** includes having integrity. Some people may never steal, but walking in pride is as bad as stealing.

▶ **If you hear** someone claim to be one of the most humble people you have ever met, or if that someone claims to have more integrity than anyone else, be cautious.

▶ **Start doing** the right thing even in small situations. Do not let little white lies slip past your lips. If you practice in the small things, you will be better prepared when big things come up.

> *The man of integrity walks securely, but he who takes crooked paths will be found out.*
> Proverbs 10:9, NIV

40 question

Why is accountability so important?

If you have ever watched the cartoon *Tom and Jerry*, you know that Tom always chases Jerry. Many times it is to prevent Jerry from eating all the food. It is easy to make Tom a villain because he seems mean, but Jerry needs Tom. If Tom did not chase Jerry and keep him from stealing all the food, Jerry would be one large mouse. In some ways, then, Jerry should thank Tom. Jerry (like everyone) needs someone to keep him accountable.

answer

Human beings often go to extremes, like being lazy or a workaholic, or eating too much or not enough, or being too insecure or too prideful. Humans are fallen and need one another to help keep them balanced. It is almost impossible to keep integrity without having accountability. If you want to do the right things the right way, you need accountability. Regardless of the reason, you will be far ahead of most people your age if you master the area of accountability.

There are various reasons why you may need accountability. You may want to lose weight, find a job, or avoid a public scandal due to an affair or a financial indiscretion. Accountability is simply having an extra set of eyes to help keep you from failing.

Here are some tips:

Submit. In America it is easy to be so independent that you do not allow anyone to speak to your life. However, if you want accountability, you will need to submit to someone whom you trust and allow him or her to speak to your life. This may be difficult if you are used to doing your own thing your own way.

Be honest. When you find someone you trust, be honest with him. If you are less than truthful, the accountability process will be less than effective. Share your strengths, weaknesses, and fears.

Listen. Listen to what your accountability partner says to you. Do not be defensive. If you are, you prevent yourself from being open to wise counsel.

worth thinking about

▶ **You do not** want to pour your heart out to just anyone. Use wisdom in choosing someone trustworthy to hold you accountable.

▶ **Accountability is necessary.** Try not to avoid this process. In the end, it is best to submit to a pastor or respected leader as soon as possible.

▶ **It is often wise** to pick someone who has success in the area in which you want to improve. This helps you learn from someone else's experience.

> *Without guidance, people fall, but with many counselors there is deliverance.*
> Proverbs 11:14, HCSB

question

▼

Who best suits your need for accountability?

If you want to have integrity and be accountable, you must figure out whom to go to for your particular needs. If you wanted to learn to tap-dance, for instance, you would not look for a plumber. That would be like asking a hammer to do the job of a feather. First, identify the area of accountability. Then, look for someone you trust who is skilled in your area of need.

answer

▼

The following are some people who can help you to address specific areas:

Mentor. Mentoring is an imparting from a leader to a follower. A mentor comes alongside you and trains and challenges you in a particular area. This is very much a teacher-student type of relationship where you allow someone to speak directly to your life. A mentor may show you the ropes on how to be a good spouse in marriage or a success in business. This is often an unofficial relationship.

Counselor. Counselors help you become more whole (oftentimes by dealing with the past) in order to move forward in your life. If you have unresolved issues in your life and need someone to talk to, you may want to see a counselor. This can be an unofficial relationship, but is most often an official relationship where you pay the counselor.

Coach. Coaching is more of a partnership where you have certain goals and the coach helps you make plans to accomplish those goals. A coach tries to draw out answers from the person he is leading in order to improve the person's decision-making abilities.

Pastor. A pastor can be any of the above. Typically, a pastor has a gift in one of these areas, so you would need to know your pastor's gifts. A pastor normally covers spiritual matters more than the other relationships.

Friend. Friends can also contribute many aspects of the preceding relationships.

worth thinking about

▶ **Be sure that** whomever you select is trustworthy. Pick someone you trust who will keep your personal business confidential.

▶ **Going to counseling** no longer carries the stigma it once did. Now it is common.

▶ **For sensitive matters,** an official relationship with someone you do not know (such as a counselor) may allow you more freedom to open up.

> *It is not only what we do, but also what we do not do, for which we are accountable.*
> Molière

42

question

▼

How do you handle temptation?

You will always have to face temptation. Adam and Eve faced it in the Garden of Eden, and you probably faced it in school. Now that you are a graduate, you will continue to face temptations. You might be tempted to take credit for a colleague's work, drink too much at an office party, or sleep with that popular person who might raise your social status. When you find yourself in a situation where you are tempted, you have to think fast. Sometimes the temptation is so quick you only have a few moments to react.

answer

▼

Temptation is not new. Joseph in the Book of Genesis was tempted to commit adultery. His response is a great template for dealing with temptation:

Acknowledge that you sin against God. You must realize that when you screw up, you affect those you care about and not just yourself. However, the biggest consideration is that you sin against God. Never trade God's blessings for a moment of pleasure. When Joseph was tempted, he pointed out that he did not want to sin against God.

Refuse. If you find yourself in a compromising situation, immediately say no. To just say no may sound simplistic, but it is better than saying yes or worse yet just saying nothing at all. Joseph said not just once, but multiple times. Most likely, you will have to refuse more than once.

Run and do not look back. If someone keeps pressuring you to do something you do not feel right about, leave immediately. Do not wait or even worry about offending the other person. Just leave. Run if need be. An adulterous woman pestered Joseph so much that he fled and even left his pants in order to get away from her.

Avoid not having support. Do your best to be around other people to avoid finding yourself in an awkward situation. The reason Joseph was caught in such a difficult situation was that none of the other house workers were present to prevent the woman from going after him.

worth thinking about

▶ **Unless it is** a high-pressure situation, do your best not to come off as stuck-up. If someone asks you if you want to smoke, simply say no thank you. Do not spout off in a condescending manner about how you do not do that and neither should they.

▶ **Keep in mind** that God really does see and know everything you do.

▶ **Many times** if you say no confidently, people do not push you. If you waffle, they will likely pressure you more. Be strong. Be decisive. Be quick to respond.

> *The eyes of the LORD are in every place,*
> *watching the evil and the good.*
> Proverbs 15:3, NAS

question

How does God speak to you?

God is not a distant God. He cares about what happens in your life, and He wants to communicate with you. Yet, because human beings often preoccupy themselves with their lives, communication is limited to their small concept of what it should be. Humanity often misses what God says. If you want God to talk to you, it is important that you know where to hear Him. When He does speak to you, listen.

answer

God speaks to you in three primary ways if you tune yourself in:

Bible. You can find the answers to 95 percent of all the big questions you have in life in the Bible. The Bible tells you how to live, how much God loves you, and how you should interact with others. The Bible gives advice on business, marriage, and forgiveness. If you take the time to read it, the Bible will answer many of your questions. God speaks to you primarily in this way. Do not seek answers elsewhere if you have not looked in the Bible first.

Personal revelation. There are some specific concerns you may encounter that the Bible does not address, concerns like which job you should take or whether you should move. In these types of situations, God often gives personal revelation as to what to do. Personal revelation, however, should never contradict the principles in the Bible. If you get a revelation to punch Sean in the nose because he upset you, that is most likely not of God.

Others. Sometimes God speaks through those around you. People who know you often see things that perhaps you do not. If their advice or input contradicts the Bible, however, it is likely not God talking to you. For instance, if your uncle tells you that you should buy one car rather than another, it may be God helping you avoid a bad decision. This is especially true if your uncle has a history of making good decisions.

worth thinking about

▶ **If you find** it difficult to understand the Bible, try to find an updated translation that makes it easier to understand.

▶ **Read a little** bit every day. Do not worry so much on the front end about how much you read, but make your Bible-reading habit a daily one.

▶ **If you do not** know where to start reading, begin with Proverbs and Romans. Since there are thirty-one days in a month, you could read one chapter of Proverbs each day.

> *How can a young person stay pure?*
> *By obeying your word.*
> Psalm 119:9, NLT

44

question

Is there only one right path to take?

The question that nearly every graduate hates to hear is this: "What are you going to do next?" Besides the fact that it gets old answering this question, many graduates do not know what they will do next and cannot stand for anyone to remind them of that. Choosing a particular path in life can be troublesome when there is more than one path. How do you know what to do? What if you make the wrong decision?

answer

People tend to squander time worrying whether they have planned everything or wondering if they will have to make their own way. The fear of making one bad decision prevents many people from doing anything. If you fear that one wrong move blots out your entire future, you will be afraid of doing anything. Instead of focusing on making the one right choice, focus on being obedient to God. The Bible is clear on how to conduct yourself in making decisions and treating people, so start there. Act with integrity and treat people the way you would want to be treated. If you do not have your future nailed down, it hardly matters if you make bad decisions in other areas. Making the right choice the wrong way is still making the wrong choice.

Feel free to make bold decisions and accept that you will likely make some wrong choices. Yet you should know that God has much grace for you. Can you imagine God getting upset because you decided to go on a mission trip to Africa? God is not in heaven shaking His head and wondering why you would be helping people in need. The same is true if you choose to paint versus becoming an investment banker. God is not biased against acrylics, and He is not biased in favor of investing. How you do things is most often more important than what you do. The Bible focuses mostly on the how and less on the what.

worth thinking about

- ▶ There are certain times when God shows specific steps to take in life, and this is why you must plug into His Word and keep in touch through prayer.

- ▶ God works all things together for good. If you make an honest mistake, take comfort in the fact that God can work even your mistakes as good things.

- ▶ Obedience is more important than perfection. Obey God by living a life according to His Word.

> *Don't you realize that you become the slave of whatever you choose to obey?*
> Romans 6:16, NLT

question

When was the last time you prayed?

When you were in school, did you have a friend who stopped talking to you? Then when you finally did address the issue, you discovered your friend thought you were the one who had stopped talking. Misunderstandings are not uncommon in school. Sometimes when you want to hear from God, you have to ask yourself when you talked to Him last. Communication with God should be dialogue and not simply monologue.

answer

An old saying goes, "If you feel distant from God, guess who moved?" This strikes right to the point that you have a responsibility to stay connected to God. People forget or avoid praying for all sorts of reasons. Sometimes it is because prayer is not a priority; other times it is because one does not know how to pray. The following are tips on how to pray:

Plan. Make time to pray every day. By being intentional, you show that prayer is a priority to you.

Praise. When you start to pray, first acknowledge how awesome God is. Some people pray only to get something or to get out of trouble. Change things up by telling God how much He means to you.

Thanks. Tell God that you are thankful for all He has given you, whether it is a home, food, clothes, a job, or even a new car. Do not wait until Thanksgiving to give thanks.

His will. Ask for God's will in your life even if it means that you do not get exactly what you want. Some people think they can demand that God do a particular thing. Instead, however, ask God to answer your prayers according to His will. In the end, you would be better off having things God's way than your own way.

Forgiveness. Ask God to forgive you for anything you may have done, and ask for help in forgiving others in your life.

Provision. Ask God for things you may need or desire. Health, safety, and other provisions are examples.

worth thinking about

▶ **Become the master** of the five-second prayer. If you are at work and something comes to mind, stop and pray quickly about it: "God, please protect Debbie while she's in Germany." Sometimes certain things come to mind because God wants you to pray for them.

▶ **The above** examples are not formulaic steps to follow but rather are simply guidelines to help you get started.

▶ **When you** pray, believe that God will hear your prayers.

> *I call on you, O God, for you will answer me;*
> *give ear to me and hear my prayer.*
> Psalm 17:6, NIV

question

▼

What if you fail?

There is a major fear of failing in the American culture, because quite often the picture of a self-made person is one where success is glorified and failure is despised. Even in high school there are awards for those most likely to succeed, most likely to become president, and most likely to clean the bathrooms of the local IHOP. There is a success hierarchy in the minds of many graduates, and most graduates do not want to end up on the wrong end of it.

answer

▼

What happens if you do everything in your power and yet you still fall on your face? Many graduates do not want to be the big dreamer who goes off to catch a dream only to return later in defeat. When dealing with the fear of failure, consider the following:

Accept failure. If you need the suspense to end, then here it is: you will fail. At some point in time you will be on the opposite end of success. It probably will not feel good. This should liberate you, because the worst thing in life is not failure; the worst thing in life is never trying. Many middle-aged people look back on life with regret because they never gave their dreams a shot. Do not hide from failure; embrace it. It means you are trying. Be okay with giving it your best shot regardless of the outcome.

Keep going. Failing once, twice, or even several dozen times does not always mean you are finished. Thomas Edison tried about a bazillion times to get his lightbulb to work, but he failed until the one light worked. Did his many attempts make him a failure?

Learn from it. Each time you fail, learn from it. Every single time, see what you could have done better, improve on it, and grow from it.

Learn from the experience of others. Watch people who are doing what you want to do, and learn from their successes. Look at what other people do wrong as well, and adjust your approach to avoid the same mistakes that others have made.

worth thinking about

▶ **Accepting failure** can sometimes be difficult, because some people do not allow themselves to accept failure. On *American Idol*, you can see thousands of wannabe singers refuse to accept their failure and instead choose to complain about the judges.

▶ **If you see** someone who is doing what you want to do, then ask him for advice. Do not be prideful or fearful to get input.

▶ **Be sure to work** hard. Do not expect the doors to open without help. The arms of hard work often open the doors of opportunity.

> *A life spent making mistakes is not only more honorable, but more useful than a life spent doing nothing.*
> George Bernard Shaw

question

Does God really care?

answer

God loved the world in this way: He gave His One and Only Son, so that everyone who believes in Him will not perish but have eternal life. For God did not send His Son into the world that He might judge the world, but that the world might be saved through Him. Anyone who believes in Him is not judged, but anyone who does not believe is already judged, because he has not believed in the name of the One and Only Son of God.

John 3:16–18, HCSB

question

What if doors of opportunity close?

You may be one of those types of people who like to plan everything out. You may even know what your next step will be now that you are done with school, but what happens if an open door of opportunity closes? It can be deflating if the one thing you really wanted to do ends up falling through. Starting from scratch is often not what you want to do, but it may be what you have to do.

answer

It is common for situations to change, and if you are not prepared to cope with that, you can find yourself wasting valuable time drowning in your own disappointment. If you find yourself in front of a closed door, do the following:

Check again. Make sure you recheck the opportunity. Be sure that the door is absolutely closed. If it is slightly ajar, or if there is even a small possibility of hope that it might reopen, keep trying. A famous story about actor and producer Danny DeVito says that he auditioned one hundred times and was told no every time. He kept at it. Finally, he was cast in the sitcom *Taxi*. If he had left after the first no, he never would have succeeded the way he has.

Review other options. Once you know that the door you wanted is closed, look at your other options. Review other schools and companies that might work even if they were not your original choice. Do more research to gather enough information to make a decision. Figure out what it was about the first door that intrigued you so much, and see if any other option comes close to it. Many times second choices end up being better than the original ones.

Move on. Start taking steps in other directions, but always stay prepared in case the door you first wanted reopens later on. If you stay prepared, you will be ready to go.

worth thinking about

▶ **Many times** when God closes one door He opens another one, so keep your eyes peeled for new doors.

▶ **Do your best** not to put all of your hope into just one option. Keeping all of your eggs in one basket often leads to major disappointment.

▶ **Recheck the first** door every six months just to see if there are new possibilities. Six months is enough time to show you are persistent without being pushy or annoying.

> *Direct me in the path of your commands,*
> *for there I find delight.*
> Psalm 119:35, NIV

question

▼

Do you have unrealistic expectations?

In these modern days of fairy tales and action movies, it is easy to form an unrealistic concept of what life should be like. In fairy tales, the hero always finds the right love and everything ends happily ever after. In action movies, even if you are shot twelve times the final scene ends with your beating the bad guys. In the real world, life can be as dramatic, but the resolutions are not quite so defined and neat.

answer

▼

If you expect life to be one big storybook, you are setting yourself up for constant failure. There is a big difference between high standards and unrealistic expectations. People often mistake the two. Here are the differences:

High standards. Having high standards is setting high values and goals in one's life. There is no problem in setting goals or wanting to live according to high standards. If you can sing, practicing hard and wanting to be the best you can be is fine. When you want to avoid drugs and alcohol because you know they can hinder your career, high standards are great guidelines. Shooting for the stars takes guts. High standards demand that you carry out goals with integrity and hold true to personal values.

Unrealistic expectations. Operating from unrealistic expectations looks a lot different. Unrealistic expectations require that you never leave room for anything less than perfection. For example, 9.8 is not good enough, because only 10.0 will do. This unrealistic outlook affects your self-esteem, those around you, and your situations. Nothing in your life can measure up to these expectations because what you think something or someone should be is not possible. You know you are operating with unrealistic expectations if you reach for the stars, get the moon instead, and are not happy with it. Unrealistic expectations are rooted in a perfectionistic mentality. Perfection is the complete absence of error, and that is nearly impossible to attain.

worth thinking about

▶ **Being optimistic** is different from having unrealistic expectations. Being optimistic is being hopeful of something or someone. Disappointment in anything less than perfection springs from unrealistic expectations.

▶ **Excellence is setting** out to do your best in every situation. Perfectionism is expecting that you have to be the best at any cost. This leads to constantly unmet expectations.

▶ **Being a perfectionist** with unrealistic expectations can strongly affect your relationships. Those around you will likely never feel good enough.

> *Striving for excellence motivates you;*
> *striving for perfection is demoralizing.*
> Harriet Braiker

question

▼

Do you value the wrong things?

What you value plays a pivotal role in what you do and how you do it. Values show you what your priorities are. Your values not only motivate you and push you to do what you do, but they are the reasons why you are pushed. Essentially, core values are the beliefs you hold dearest, beliefs such as integrity, family, and love. Core values influence your thoughts, thoughts influence your emotions, and your emotions influence your actions. If you are guided by the wrong values, your whole life will be out of whack.

answer

▼

For example, if you value money and you do not have any, then you think you have nothing, feel as though you have nothing, and may end up arguing with loved ones due to your low self-esteem. This starts a cycle of depression, all because you based your self-worth on faulty values. How do you get your values on the right track? Here are some ideas:

God's business. The Bible says to put God's kingdom first. If you look at your values compared to what the Bible says, you can see if you are doing so. In fact, the Bible says that if you seek after His kingdom first, all the extra stuff will be added to you. You have to figure out if you are chasing after the "extra" stuff first rather than God's concept of what is important. This does not mean that a pastor is better in God's eyes than a plumber is. It means that if you value status more than prayer or influence and more than giving to people in need, you are going after the wrong things.

Righteousness. Another way to check your values is to see if you are seeking upright and moral living. The Bible says that you should seek God's righteousness. This means that you should pursue His concept of right and wrong and not your own. Humanity has all sorts of concepts of right and wrong, but God's concepts are the ones you should seek after.

worth thinking about

▶ **Do not be** like some people who try to make deals with God by saying that if God will allow them this achievement or that amount of money, they will do what they know is right.

▶ **Most of the time** if you do not do what is right now, you will likely not do it later. Procrastination is the second cousin to apathy.

▶ **God's concept** of right and wrong is not legalistic, but neither is it relative, allowing you to do what you want when you want.

> *Seek first his kingdom and his righteousness, and all these things will be given to you as well.*
> Matthew 6:33, NIV

50

question

What is the opposite of failure?

You may think the answer to this question is easy. However, if you think the answer is success, you are wrong. Success is not the opposite of failure. Many people are successful but nonetheless miserable and unhappy. Glances at Hollywood, Wall Street, and Capitol Hill will show you many people who were successful in their goals but failures in life. The true opposite of failure is joy.

answer

Being able to experience real joy in life brings contentment, love, and passion. Failure brings fear, depression, and eventually anger. The more you run from it, the more failure can act like a fire and consume you, so fight the fire with the familiar stop, drop, and roll:

Stop. Stop worrying about failing. Stop comparing yourself to other people you know or even to people you do not know. Stop holding yourself over a barrel of inadequacy. Stop. By stopping, you allow yourself to relax and think for a moment. Worrying about success is a never-ending treadmill run. You keep going and going, but you do not get anywhere and end up exhausted after the fact.

Drop. Drop your concept of success. Put down that weight of expectation, and take a deep breath. You may find out that you enjoy life a bit more without all that extra baggage. You will never find true success at the top of the mountain. Success comes in the hike up the mountain, so enjoy it.

Roll. Roll around on the ground and laugh. Seriously, just goof off for a second. When you constantly worry about being the best and achieving everything, it is hard to enjoy what you are doing. It is okay to want to go after a goal, but it is not okay to do so miserably. Take joy in what you are doing whether you win, lose, or draw. If you do not enjoy what you are doing, you probably will not enjoy the long haul anyhow.

worth thinking about

▶ **Many times**, people achieve their goals once they stop obsessing about success. Letting go can sometimes be tough, but often it pays off.

▶ **If you do not** know how to stop worrying, then stop what you are doing and get a massage. You may even want to go camping or take a weekend trip to some small obscure town to get away.

▶ **If you have** no idea how to have fun, go to a circus, zoo, or anywhere kids are.

> *A joyful heart is good medicine, but a broken spirit dries up the bones.*
> Proverbs 17:22, NAS

51 question

How do you define success?

Whether you view your life as a success or a failure largely hinges on what you view as the pinnacle of life. When answering this question you should look at it from the finish line and not the beginning. When you are on your deathbed will you think, *Man, I wish I had worked ten more hours a week*? Probably not. Most people in their last few minutes on earth wish they had spent more time with their friends and family.

answer

Workaholics yearn for the time they wasted, estranged family members lament the words they have said, and the rich realize the money they made will soon no longer be under their control. Sixty or seventy years from now, what will you wish you had done? If you truly want to be successful:

Make family your priority. When you start to have a family, make sure you place them at the top of your to-do list. Treat your spouse as the real treasure. One of God's greatest gifts to you is someone to walk along with you and give testimony of your life. Funny inside jokes and triumphs are hollow when there is no one to walk the road with you. No boss or fan will ever give better rewards than children who know they are the center of your world. The rewards of family last forever, because after you die your family will pass on the love you gave them. That book you wrote, film you produced, or song you sang will fade from memory, but family love will pass on forever.

Build a strong sense of community. Do not focus only on your family. Spend time with your neighbors, church group, or fellow parents in the PTA. Studies show that people who are married and go to church have a higher quality of life than those who do not. Studies also show that smaller communities tend to have a higher quality of life than the busy cities. No doubt, this is connected to the emphasis of community in smaller towns.

worth thinking about

▶ By being involved in your local church and not going just on Sunday, you can build a strong sense of community.

▶ Make sure your spouse is top priority. Two parents who make each other priorities are far more loving and have more to offer their children.

▶ Do your best to attend as many of your children's ball games and dance recitals as you possibly can. No manager or obligation is important enough to miss them.

> *I don't care how poor a man is;*
> *if he has family, he's rich.*
> Dan Wilcox and Thad Mumford

question

Do you fear the opinions
of others?

You only have to be on the wrong side of a vicious rumor once to become fearful of what others might say about you. People can sometimes just be downright mean in the things they say. "Loose Lips Lori," "Gossipy Gertrude," and "Lying Lenny" can make life difficult. Even when some folks have good intentions, however, you still may fear their opinions of you. They could be family, friends, or even strangers.

answer

If you like to be liked, you should know now that not everyone will like you all of the time. Even if people seem nice to your face, at some point other people will think unkindly about you. Do not beat yourself up about it. Sometimes it helps to know why, so here are a few reasons:

Jealousy. Sometimes people want to have everything and be the best. If you are better or have something (or someone) other people want, some people are going to accuse you of being a jerk or a nag. These people do not rise to a higher level; they prefer tearing others down to their level.

Expectations. They may have expectations about you that you may not meet. If they want your attention or time but you give them to other people, they can feel that you let them down. People with unrealistic expectations often place blame on those who do not measure up to their standards.

Gossip. Others just like to hear a good story. As long as it does not involve them personally, they just love to hear and spread interesting stories. After a while truth and fiction get blurry.

Differences. Then there are people who are simply different from you. They have different personalities and cultural norms. If you are different, people sometimes think of you as flawed. If you are outgoing, people sometimes think of you as too boisterous and loud. Different is not bad; it is just different.

worth thinking about

▶ **Be cautious** that you do not do to others what others may do to you. Do not judge or slander those whom you do not like. Treat others even better than you would want to be treated.

▶ **Do not feel** you must change simply because you are not what others want you to be. Growth is healthy, but growth is not necessarily conformity.

▶ **If you constantly** change for other people, you will never know who you are.

> *He who goes about as a slanderer reveals secrets, therefore do not associate with a gossip.*
> Proverbs 20:19, NAS

53

question

How do you keep from giving up?

At some point or another when you were in school, you probably had thoughts about giving up. Maybe the work seemed too hard, too boring, or too much. However, you kept going, and you have indeed graduated. But what happens when you hit the wall? What if you are lost in the woods and know that you are on the same path you were ninety-seven laps ago, and there doesn't seem to be any hope of getting beyond those stumps of repetition?

answer

The thought of giving up can come on subtly in the midst of yet another failed attempt. After a while, making a distinct change in direction can even start to sound logical. Yet if you want to persevere, do the following:

Be consistently precise. Always be on time, never miss a meeting, and do everything you possibly can to position yourself for the desire in your heart. Rather than be a sledgehammer that tries to get everything in one swing, be a chisel that is precise but constant. Be a sharpshooter that eschews buckshot.

Set up reminders. If you are down on your luck, keep in mind what your end game is. If you want to be an actor, put up a poster of the movie that inspired you. If you want to be a professional athlete, place an autographed picture of Barry Sanders next to your bed. If you want a raise more than anything, tape your goals on the dashboard of your car. Keep hope alive by never losing sight of your dream.

Take a risk. If you have been at a job for a long time and nothing has changed, do something you have not tried. If you want your boss to notice you at work, develop a proposal that might help your company and pitch it to your boss. If you want to publish a book, save up and go to that writer's conference. Take a risk.

worth thinking about

▶ **Failures are often** lessons for later. Learning is a process, and many times the longer the wait, the greater the actual enjoyment of the success. Those who hit the jackpot right away often never learn to appreciate the mountaintop.

▶ **No matter** how tough it gets, do not lose your passion.

▶ **Do your best** no matter what. It can be easy to drag your feet when you feel as though nothing you do matters anyway. Do not give in to that rut.

> *You need to persevere so that when you have done the will of God, you will receive what he has promised.*
> Hebrews 10:36, NIV

question

What are you passionate about?

In northern winters, the cold can take a toll on your car. The wind explodes across your path, and the frigid temperatures can sap the juice out of anyone or anything. This is never truer than when you turn the car key only to hear the most frightening noise one can hear in the midst of such cold conditions: silence. A dead car on a cold night is more than annoying; it can be deadly.

answer

This is true not only for vehicles; it is also true for people. When you let your personal battery drain due to the some-times-harsh conditions of everyday life, you can become weak and sick, and you can even lose hope. Some things can reenergize you, but few are as effective as plugging into a personal passion. Finding and doing what you are passionate about gives you power to handle other aspects of your life. Remember the mnemonic P-O-W-E-R:

Passion. Identify your passion. What is it that charges your battery as nothing else can? It may be something creative like drawing or writing. Perhaps it is organizing and planning. Whatever it is, discover it.

Opportunity. Look for ways to do the things for which you have a passion. Look around your church, in the local paper, or even online. See where you can do the things that reenergize you.

Will. Will yourself to be attentive to those activities that give you that extra boost. Oftentimes when you plug into the passions of your life, you have even more energy for the areas of your life that are less exciting.

Energize. Energize those around you to do the things for which you have a passion. Do not focus only on your passions, but use your renewed hope and fire to encourage those around you to follow your example.

Relish. Relish the time you have in the areas that recharge you. When you take time to appreciate your passions, it helps build a reserve for times that can be draining.

worth thinking about

▶ **If you do** not know what you are passionate about, then try new things. Audition for a play. Try out for the softball team. Discover your passion.

▶ **Being active** with things that you are passionate about does not mean you should do only what you like.

▶ **Many times** when people consistently work in jobs that do not play to their passions, they burn out quicker than those who do.

> *One person with passion is better than forty people merely interested.*
>
> E. M. Forster

55

question

What do you want to do?

What if you combined the wishes from all those shooting stars, the past several birthday cakes, newfound lucky pennies, and the genie in that old lamp you found under your grandma Harriet's bed and could wish that you could do exactly what you wanted? Every person needs a purpose in life, so what do you wish yours to be? Many people never take a shot at what they truly want to do. Look at your talent and your interests to decide what you want.

answer

Obviously, magic wishing does not make something happen. Thinking about what you would wish for, however, may help you identify what you like doing. When evaluating what you want to do in the future, consider the following:

Talent. Do you have the talent to be able to do what you want to do? You can develop some skills, and you either have or do not have others. If you want to be a runway supermodel, you would need to be tall, and height is not something you can control. You can develop most talents, however. Notice your talents and the seeds of your talents, and nurture them.

Knowledge. If you want to be the CEO of a major corporation, you have to train and go to school, learn people skills, learn business tactics, and groom an understanding of emerging business trends. If you want to do something, you have to study and learn in order to accomplish your goals.

Season. Be aware of which stage of life you are in. Every life goes through peaks and valleys, so be aware of the time in which you live. When you are single, you often have more freedom to take chances. When you have children, it might not be a good time to go skydiving or to enter into a risky business deal. You may not be able to do precisely what you want, but if the season is appropriate, you might think about giving it a shot.

worth thinking about

▶ **Be honest with** yourself when evaluating your talents, but do not sell yourself short.

▶ **Be sure to study** in a field related to what you really want to do, because quite often your knowledge level is where you will find work. If you are good with cars and bad with fashion, you might not get work as a designer.

▶ **There is nothing** wrong with studying multiple areas of interest. One area can be a field that you really enjoy, while another can serve as a backup plan if the first does not work out.

> *If you can't excel with talent,*
> *triumph with effort.*
> Dave Weinbaum

question

▼

How do you keep hope alive?

It is good to dream; in fact, there are times when it is vital to dream. You will be disappointed from time to time, however. There will even be times when you feel like giving up because others constantly reject or chronically ignore you. To think big is to hold out hope. Hope optimistically believes the best is yet to come. Hope is seeing the glass as half full rather than half empty.

answer

▼

Many times people lose hope because what is right in front of them catches them up. Because they cannot see beyond their own failures or disappointments, they cannot see the whole picture. It would be like standing in front of a scrapheap without looking beyond it to see the ocean. Sometimes you have to set your stuff aside and look beyond your personal letdowns. In order to keep hope alive, you must be O-T-H-E-R-focused:

Optimism. Stay positive no matter what. Keep a good attitude about your situation and about others. If you experience personal failure, you may be tempted to view others through a cynical and pessimistic lens.

Talk affirmatively. Convey to others words of affirmation in the areas of their involvement. Positive words from you can make a major difference in the life of someone else.

Help others. Help other people pursue their dreams. Invest in the people around you, and help them get a leg up. Try to develop a team mentality with the people you care about so that their success can be yours as well.

Express availability. Express to those around you that you are open and available if they need you. Most people find it difficult to ask for help, so put it out there for them.

Resist negativity. Resist worrying about what you do not have, and instead be thankful for what you do have. Negativity is a disease that spreads to those with whom you come in contact.

worth thinking about

▶ **Being optimistic** does not mean you should be unrealistic. Be realistic about your situation, but never settle for mediocrity.

▶ **Many times when** you help others, doors open for you as well. This should not be why you help others, but merely a by-product of it.

▶ **You may find** that investing in others was what you were missing to begin with. Many times helping someone else with his problems is far more rewarding than simply getting what you want.

> *Hope deferred makes the heart sick,*
> *but desire fulfilled is a tree of life.*
> Proverbs 13:12, NAS

Do I actually have to interact with people I don't like?

If you love only those who love you, what reward is there for that? Even corrupt tax collectors do that much. If you are kind only to your friends, how are you different from anyone else? Even pagans do that.

Matthew 5:46–47, NLT

question

Do you really want what you think you want?

Do you want to be a politician, actor, dancer, or professional athlete? What would your dream job be? The thing about dreams is that you can end them whenever you decide you want to do something else. If you dream of going off on wild and crazy adventures, you can do so without the threat of getting hurt, but in real life, the stakes are much higher. Do you really want what you think you want?

answer

If you want to date the most attractive, popular, and charismatic person in school, you might be disappointed if that so-labeled ideal person turns out to be self-absorbed and hot-tempered. In twenty years, will you want that person to parent your kids?

Many times people dream of something spectacular only to find out that the dream is really a nightmare. In cartoons, you might find a character who finds a genie willing to grant three wishes. The character wishes for a million dollars and gets it, but then realizes the money came from a bank, the cops discover he has the money, and he ends up in jail. It is cause and effect. If you really want what you think you want, do the following:

Count the costs. See what you have to give up to obtain what you want. If you want to go into a field with a lot of public recognition, then much of your personal and family privacy goes out the window. CEOs and presidents of corporations spend far more time dealing with work than investing in their families. If you want a strong family life, you might not always jump at every promotion. Are you willing to take that path?

Check your motives. Some people pursue goals to please or satisfy others. Be sure that your motives are yours; otherwise, you will likely end up regretting it in the future.

worth thinking about

- ▶ **Some careers** come with high costs to your personal life, so if there are other options that you enjoy just as much, you may want to consider them.

- ▶ **When you go** after a goal because someone else wants it, it may not be your own passion. Living through others can lead to unhappy endings.

- ▶ **If you are okay** with the costs, then pursue what you want, but it is always good to know what you are getting into beforehand.

> *From everyone who has been given much, much will be demanded; and from the one who has been entrusted with much, much more will be asked.*
> Luke 12:48, NIV

question

How can you be original?

It is difficult to keep up with fashions and fads because they change so rapidly. From hair to personality, people often copy someone else. You, however, do not have to be a clone—a cheaper, lesser version of someone else's idea. You are, and deserve for others to recognize you as, an original.

answer

Clothes and fashion can be helpful, but in order to stand out, you must first *be* different rather than simply *look* different. Here are some guidelines to being O-R-I-G-I-N-A-L:

Own mistakes. The norm is to shift the blame to someone else. People often are reluctant to own their mistakes. Most blame shifting is done out of fear, so buck up and own your faults.

Respect authority. Respect those above you rather than criticize them. Leaders notice the people who show them respect (even when they do not deserve it). Showing respect often breeds respect.

Ignore gossip. Ignore the watercooler talk, because most of what you hear is untrue, and half of what you see is not true, either. The last thing you want is to have your name attached to a little piece of hearsay that makes its way around the office or campus.

Give. Give more than you get. People do not reach success by themselves. At some point, someone helped them along the way. In both success and failure, give to others. The more money, resources, and wisdom you have, the more you should give to others.

Invite God. Invite God into your everyday life—and not only when you are in trouble or getting ready to eat dinner.

No favoritism. Do not favor people based on social status or influence.

Avoid groupthink. Do not think like everyone else simply to gain approval of others. Seek your own answers.

Laugh. Be joyful—too many people are cynical and depressed.

worth thinking about

- ▶ **If you become** a billionaire, a few thousand bucks is not very much. If you are successful, do not pinch pennies in giving to others.

- ▶ **Some look** at happy, joyful people as unaware and naive, but this is because many do not have joy in their lives. Stand out by keeping a smile on your face.

- ▶ **Respecting authority** does not mean being a doormat. It is okay to stand up for standards and principles.

> *A stingy man is eager to get rich and is unaware that poverty awaits him.*
> Proverbs 28:22, NIV

question

▼

Are there dream slayers in your life?

For every one person who reaches the height of his or her dream, ten thousand others fall far short of their aspirations. Those who fail often try to keep others from succeeding. Either from fear or jealousy, some people like to prevent others from treading paths that they once hoped to tread. These people always say that landing on the moon is impossible. Somewhere along the way, their dream got derailed.

answer

▼

Some dream slayers have good intentions. Failure to attain their goals likely hurt some. Others simply want to hold you down so that you do not surpass what they have done. Getting wise input is important, but you need to be able to recognize if those from whom you seek advice have your best interests in mind. You would not ask Biff the Bully whether he thought you were a high-quality person, would you? He would likely steal your lunch money and then spew choice words about the less-than-stellar qualities of your family tree. When looking at the people around you and the advice they offer, consider the following:

Do your dream slayers base their opinions in fear? Fear in itself should not dictate your future. Consider things that may be concerns, but do not avoid doing something simply because of fear. If your parents do not want you to move simply because they will not be there, that is not a convincing reason. Now if you plan on moving but have no money, no plan, and no relational support and have never done anything alone, then you might want to rethink your approach.

Do your dream slayers oppose your plans out of jealousy? One way to know this is to ask yourself if this person gets excited for you when you do well. Another way is to ask yourself if this person cheers you on in your pursuits. If he is competitive with you, then you might take what he says with a grain of salt.

worth thinking about

- ▶ If you do rethink your approach to moving, this does not mean that you should not move, but it does mean that you might want to rethink your plans for moving.

- ▶ Identifying another's motives as arising from jealousy is tough because you cannot see another's intentions, but you can see that person's history of support for you and the things you do.

- ▶ It is okay to listen to what others have to say by weighing their words carefully to determine if they are basing their insights in fear or jealousy.

> *You can go to bed without fear;*
> *you will lie down and sleep soundly.*
> Proverbs 3:24, NLT

question
▼

Can you crawl before you walk?

Have you ever wondered what life would be like if the moment you were born you had jumped out of the delivery room and run down the hallways yelling at everyone, announcing that you had just been born? It is a funny thought, but babies are just not born with the ability to walk and talk, let alone to know the integral dynamics of self-promotion. The reality is that you have to crawl before you can sprint down a hallway.

answer
▼

If you want to take the world by storm and leave a lasting impression with your life, realize that most of the time you do not start on top. Do not despise humble beginnings. They are often the basis of the most compelling stories. America especially admires the underdog. Work hard and see a humble start as a challenge and not a defeat. If you want to be a top-dog manager, then serving coffee as an intern may not be a bad idea. Work your tail off and earn your stripes. Respect is not automatic; you earn it. As you grow from crawling to running, adopt the D-A-N principle:

Defer gratification. Do not live now the way you want to live tomorrow. Live now so you can live how you want tomorrow. This means to save the expensive stuff for when you have the money to do it. Do not buy all of the stuff you want immediately. Save these things as rewards for climbing the organization ladder. By deferring gratification early, you keep yourself out of debt so you can have freedom down the road when you really need credit.

Allow room for failure. Accept the fact that you will make mistakes. Give yourself room, and learn from your mistakes. This will help you take a few chances from time to time.

Never compromise values. Know what you believe, and do not go against your beliefs in order to get ahead. If you do, it will be more difficult to enjoy your success.

worth thinking about

▶ When you start on top, you have nowhere to go but down. When you have to work for your goals, you appreciate them more.

▶ Learn from your failures, but also learn from others what not to do. If you can sidestep a problem, do so by learning from those around you.

▶ Be sure to take time to figure out your personal values so that you can make decisions according to them in the future.

> *A man will not be established by wickedness, but the root of the righteous will not be moved.*
> Proverbs 12:3, NAS

61 question

What do you want to do before you die?

Despite the fact that you just graduated, it is not too soon to think of the things you want to do before you die. There are several times in your life that you will have to take risks in order to pursue your heart's desires. This requires faith. A checklist can help guide you, and when you do something on the list, check it off.

answer

In Genesis, Abraham set forth a good example of how to take a step of faith. To build up your faith so that you can take steps toward your heart's desires, do the following:

Pass the tests. Challenging times will test you, so do the right thing. God will reward you in the end.

Act immediately. Do not drag your feet when it is time to do something. Act right away. Doing the right thing late is often a form of disobedience.

Do not neglect basic needs. If you have a specific task, do not neglect the basic needs. Some people become so caught up in glitz and glamour that they overlook the foundational necessities.

Wade through loneliness. Sometimes when you step out on faith, you will find yourself all alone. This is not a sign to give up. It is simply a sign that you have to do some things on your own.

Stand strong in faith. When others question what you are doing, keep holding on to faith when you know you are doing the right thing.

Do what you know. If you do not know what else you need to do, do what you know to do.

Be attentive. Do not become distracted. Stay aware of open doors, provision, or God's nudging.

Worship and remember. Worship God, and remember what He has done for you. This helps build up your faith for future trials.

worth thinking about

▶ Just about every great thing in life requires a person to have a great deal of faith. Abraham and Abraham Lincoln had to have faith.

▶ If you do not do anything when you do not know what to do, you become stagnate. Doing what you know to do at least keeps you active and often opens potential doors of opportunity.

▶ Do not be a procrastinator. Practice acting immediately. Start and finish homework and work projects before they are due.

> *Faith is being sure of what we hope for and certain of what we do not see.*
> Hebrews 11:1, NIV

62 question

What did you want to be as a kid?

The daydreams of yesteryear can be refreshing. When you were a kid, your only responsibility was to have fun and stay out of the cookie jar. Everything seemed more black and white. You played cops and robbers or had tea parties where everyone had manners or you may even have made the cops and robbers play tea party with you. The dreams of a child reflect the heart that beats within the child.

answer

Now that you have graduated, people have probably asked about your plans and goals. Most of the askers likely gave you their personal opinions on what you should do. The questions, and the expectations that go along with the questions, assume you know what your entire life should look like. Maybe you liked playing cowboys and Indians in the woods next to your home with your friend Justin. Hiding in the trees or under the freshly fallen leaves was a rush.

Do you get the same rush working in an office nine to five with a half-hour lunch break? Some do, but many do not. As you approach the rest of your life, plug into what your heart desires. Maybe you do not enjoy the big-business lifestyle and the hectic overload it can sometimes impose. Perhaps you loved doing church plays as a kid. It can be easy to lose touch with your heart's true desires. Maybe you are suited to be involved in your church arts program.

Your dream may not make the big bucks. But was it your dream to forgo creativity for constant business? Take notice of the games you played as a kid. If you do, you can find the seeds of not only what you want, but also maybe what you are good at. Did you like to play grocery store and organize things to make them nice and efficient? This might make you a good manager. Everyone is different.

worth thinking about

- ▶ Do not downplay your desires as a kid, because they often show you what you really wanted to do before the questions and responsibility came.

- ▶ Childhood dreams may not be complete, however. If you love to play sports and enjoy teamwork but lack the talent to make a career out of playing, then maybe coaching or some related field would fill that desire.

- ▶ Less money and a joyful, fulfilled heart are better than a miserable but wealthy life.

> I tell you the truth, unless you change and become like little children, you will never enter the kingdom of heaven.
> Matthew 18:3, NIV

63 — **question**

How do you help parents let go?

Saying good-bye to gym class, bad cafeteria food, and Ms. Thornville from literature class is the easy part. Saying good-bye to Mom and Dad is more difficult. As children grow up, many parents hold on tighter for fear of losing their little boy or girl. You may embrace or resent this fact, but it is important for you as a young adult to handle this transition with maturity and sensitivity.

answer

Graduates tend to have two very different thoughts on cutting the apron strings. Either they cannot wait until they are out on their own, or they cling ever so tightly to their parents. Which are you? Are you champing at the bit to gain your independence? Alternatively, do you want to hold on to the safety your parents provide?

If you are the type that clings to your parents, it is important to know that having a strong relationship with your mom and dad is not a bad thing. In fact, many people probably wish they had the same relationship. However, a couple of things need to happen. As a graduate, getting out on your own and getting a job are necessary. It is time to carry your own weight.

If you are the type who cannot wait to get away from your parents, it is important to note that it is okay to want to get out on your own. How you do it is also important. Try to put yourself in their shoes. Your parents likely have made many sacrifices for you to be able to graduate, so be sure to show your appreciation now as you become more independent. How do you do this? Start by acknowledging your parents' sacrifices. Let them know how much you appreciate them. Listen to them, even if you have heard the story or their advice a hundred times. Listen.

worth thinking about

▶ **As you become** more independent, be sure to ask your dad for advice or help. Males have a strong need to feel needed. If your dad is good with cars, go to him for advice if you have car troubles, even if this means calling him from a thousand miles away. He will appreciate it.

▶ **Call and e-mail** your mom on a regular basis. Your mom wants to know you love her. You can never tell her enough.

▶ **Remember important** family dates like birthdays and anniversaries.

> *Let your father and your mother be glad,*
> *and let her rejoice who gave birth to you.*
> Proverbs 23:25, NAS

question

Why keep in touch with friends?

The world has become more transitory over the past few decades. Travel is easier and more common. It is becoming rarer and rarer for an individual to live an entire lifetime in one town, with one community and one way of life. Change has become the norm, and with transitions looming it is important to keep in touch with those you care about. This requires work on your part.

answer

Some friends are merely activity friends. These are people who are in the same class, on the same team, or in some other activity that brings them together. Soon after the activity ends, the relationships also end. Lifelong friends transcend activities. You care about these people, and they care about you. These types of friends do not just pop up like magic. Like any solid relationship, you must maintain them. As you get older, you will become more aware that good friends are hard to find. You cannot treat solid friendships like pieces of your wardrobe to be replaced whenever you feel like it.

Meet friends where they are. Do not always demand your relationship be on your terms. Your friendships should not be dictatorships. Care about what your friends like and need. If they like to talk things out, then do it.

If Frank is introverted, then give him space when he needs it. Do not always dictate when, where, and how you meet. Let him suggest a restaurant or two. Friendships require investments. This means time, energy, and sometimes money. When someone dumps Ann, you may need to take her out to get milk shakes.

Down the road you may need a friend to help you, too. You may hit a rough patch and need a shoulder to cry on, an ear to listen, or even a helping hand to open a few doors of opportunity to help you get back on your feet.

worth thinking about

▶ **In a day** of cell phones, e-mail, and social Web sites, there is really no reason why you cannot keep up with your friends.

▶ **Return your calls** and e-mails as soon as possible. Do not be a communication snob by ignoring or forgetting to stay in touch. Few things are as important as catching up with a friend.

▶ **Out of sight** should not be out of mind. If you have this mentality, you will get lonely quickly.

> *A friend loves at all times,*
> *and a brother is born for adversity.*
> Proverbs 17:17, NAS

65

question

Can you let go of bad influences?

Not everyone you consider your friend is a true friend. Evaluate the people around you and decide whether they are people with whom you should associate. Few things can derail you faster than unhealthy relationships with unhealthy people. Walking away from harmful relationships might be a tough decision for you to make, but it beats the alternative.

answer

Here are some suggestions for deciding whether to alter your friendships:

ATM seekers. A friend may sometimes need a helping hand with money, and there is no problem with that. You may go through tough times, too. However, if your friendship hinges on whether you give Mike money, it is not a real friendship. Being used by someone is not the definition of friendship.

Trouble seekers. If Ryan and Candace want to break the law and stir up trouble, stay away from them. If they go down, they will take you down, too. Several professional athletes have this problem. Friends from their youth get them in trouble, and it often costs them their reputations, their money, and their careers.

Gossip seekers. There are many Jefferson Jabbermouths and Betty Backstabbers who have a thirst for gossip. They know everything about everyone and love to spread what they know to others. This is how they make friends. People like being around them because they spill the beans on everyone else. Friends like these cannot be trusted, unless you want your business known by the world.

Mirror breakers. Mirror breakers like to tear down your self-image no matter what you do. You will likely never please some of those close to you. Stop spending relational energy on people who make it their goal to treat you unfairly. Mirror breakers are also the friends who never let you live down past mistakes you have made.

worth thinking about

▶ Do not let mirror breakers dictate who you are now. Do not become like them. Give others the benefit of the doubt, because others can change just as you can.

▶ There are some people you cannot just stop being around, such as family and colleagues. In these cases, simply adjust the amount you reveal and invest in them.

▶ Be aware of those who play to your weaknesses. If you struggle with alcohol and David keeps pressuring you to drink, stay away from him.

> *Leave the presence of a fool, or you will not discern words of knowledge.*
> Proverbs 14:7, NAS

66

Do you know whom you should listen to?

Everybody has an opinion, anecdote, or personal experience to sway your decisions, but not every insight is of equal value. As the mountain of insights pile up, you will need to sort through them to make a solid decision. Otherwise, an avalanche of solutions can fall in around you and prevent you from doing anything. You need to know whom to listen to and whom not to listen to.

answer

Some people, of course, can give you good words of advice, but then there are others who have drippy-faucet mouths—they make a lot of noise but do little good. Here are some guidelines for knowing whom to listen to:

Your best interests. You should at least listen to those who have your best interests in mind. This does not always mean they know what they are talking about, but at least you know they mean well.

Who benefits. Be aware of who benefits from certain decisions. Be leery if Pastor Stan decides God's purpose in your life is to work in his ministry, even if your heart is to be in business. Stan may see your talent and want it for the church. A person wanting your skills is not bad, but that person should be open to your heart's desires, too.

Have they ever done it? If you want to be a missionary and your friends do not understand why, do not fret about it. This is especially true if they have never been farther than ten miles from where their parents live. Make sure that you listen to people who have some experience in the areas you are deciding on.

Look to outside sources. It is good to listen to those close to you, but also ask the opinions of those you trust who are a bit outside your inner circle. Sometimes the perceptions of people close to you are skewed, and you might not get an accurate picture of reality.

worth thinking about

▶ **In tough times,** you can go to the people who have your best interests at heart.

▶ **Some young people** make the mistake of listening to only their friends, but many of those friends are young and have little experience in which to form their opinions. Just because someone is a friend doesn't mean he knows what he is talking about.

▶ **Some families cannot** see talent in front of them, and others see talent when it is not there.

> *The way of a fool is right in his own eyes,*
> *but a wise man is he who listens to counsel.*
> Proverbs 12:15, NAS

Is compromise that big of a deal?

Do not love this world nor the things it offers you, for when you love the world, you do not have the love of the Father in you.

For the world offers only a craving for physical pleasure, a craving for everything we see, and pride in our achievements and possessions. These are not from the Father, but are from this world.

And this world is fading away, along with everything that people crave. But anyone who does what pleases God will live forever.

1 John 2:15–17, NLT

question
▼
What if others stereo-type who you are?

Much of what you believe about yourself likely comes from other people. Studies show that birth order even plays a role in personality and characteristics. People interact with you a certain way depending on whether you are a firstborn, a middle-born, or a last-born. People often see firstborns as responsible, while they see last-borns as the fun ones. Sometimes these characteristics turn out to be true, but not always.

answer
▼

It is easier for people to sum you up into one category, so if you are a jock, it does not matter as much if you are a brain, too. You are a jock. Stereotypes are finite boxes that society places on others for purposes of better understanding and interacting. However, you are not just a small box; you are a unique individual. Some people never step out of their boxes for fear that others might look upon them as though they had five heads. "People pleasing" is the disease that keeps people imprisoned in their boxes.

You may be smart, and because you are smart, perhaps your family wants you to become a doctor. All of your older siblings became doctors. Yet you want to do something different with your life. If you want to please others, you may never take a step outside your plain cubicle. Living your life only as others want you to ensures that you likely never will be what you were meant to be. Your purpose in life is unique and given to you by a creative God. A committee of naysayers did not set forth your purpose. If you have naysayers in your life, here are some tips:

Learn to say no. Your people-pleasing ways may not stop until you learn to say no.

Accept reactions. When you say no, you may get a whole slew of negative reactions, but do not fear them.

Take action. Take a step toward what your heart is telling you to do.

worth thinking about

- ▶ **Avoid living** a life in fear of the opinions of others; do not let others make your decisions.

- ▶ **When saying no**, do not act prideful or superior. Do so with respect and reverence.

- ▶ **If you are** stereotyped, do not neglect the skills and qualities that people do see. If you are smart but want to be known as creative, do not overlook your intelligence.

> *Today you are you, that is truer than true. There is no one alive who is youer than you.*
> Dr. Seuss

question

How do you say good-bye?

Endings cap off one season of life while beckoning a new one. Some good-byes are difficult and emotional. Others are quick and deliberate. Good-byes can say a lot about a person, so it is important to handle them well. Good-byes are not only about you, but they are also about those whom you are leaving. Even if good-byes are difficult for you to handle, say them with your heart in words and actions.

answer

You want your good-bye to be memorable in a positive way. When you and others look back at your good-byes, let it be with joy and love. Here are some guidelines to help you say good-bye well:

Say good-bye. Some people do not like saying good-bye. It can often be difficult to say, but if you do not say it, you are robbing others of a sense of closure. Keep others in mind when you say your good-byes. While saying good-bye might not ease the pain of letting go, not saying good-bye makes it more difficult. If there is a going-away party, go to it. Shake hands, give hugs, and return smiles to those who care about you.

Finish strong. If you know change is around the corner, do not just drop your responsibilities. Finish what you have started, and do your best work. The last thing you want to do is to leave a bitter taste in people's mouths by dropping the ball and making others clean up the messes you leave behind. If you finish strong, you set yourself up for a strong start in the next phase of life.

Acknowledge your inner circle. You may have a lot of people to say good-bye to, but give special time to those closest to you. Immediate family and close friends should have a good amount of your time since they have likely given much of their own time to you. Let them know how much they mean to you.

worth thinking about

▶ **Do not be** in such a rush to get wherever you are going that you overlook the importance of your good-byes.

▶ **If there are words** you know you need to say, then do so before you leave. You and your loved ones are not sure what the future holds, so make sure to share your heart.

▶ **When good-byes** are tough, remember that they are not always final. If good-byes are too easy for you, remember that they might be final.

> *How lucky I am to have something that makes saying good-bye so hard.*
> Carol Sobieski and Thomas Meehan

question

▼

Who are you?

This is one of the most difficult questions for many people to answer, because most people do not know who they really are. You can look at the roles you play, your personality, and what others say you are and still not get the full picture of who you are. Some people judge who you are by what you do, and there is some merit to that. What you do often reveals who you are, but it is not the entire picture.

answer

▼

You may be a son, a daughter, a brother, a roommate, a husband, a wife, a mother, a father, or a regional manager of a bank, but a title comes up short in answering who you really are. It is important to look at all the hats you wear because they can reflect your heart. If you are a big sister to a young girl and you mentor her, then that definitely reveals much of what you are, but it is not you entirely. To know who you are, you must look at how God views you:

You are special. God allowed His only Son to be stretched out on a cross for your sins. That means you have to be important to Him. God sees your beauty and value and was willing to put Himself in harm's way so you could have a chance at a decent future. Can you believe that? God thought you were important enough to give you a better life and offer you a ticket into heaven.

You are capable. You have the ability to do mighty things. God says that anything is possible if you believe in Him. That means you can accomplish all sorts of things if you put your mind to it and have faith.

You are imperfect. Though you are special, you are also flawed. You are imperfect along with every other human being. Some people think that goodness comes from humanity, but God is the source of everything good, so keep that in mind. Good things come from God. Bad things do not.

worth thinking about

▶ **Despite your social** level on earth, you are royalty if you accept God's sacrifice.

▶ **Never take other** people's words over what God says about you. Some people will try to make you believe you are less than you are. Others will build you up to be greater than you are.

▶ **A true and healthy** identity cannot stand apart from God. All other self-concepts have their basis in distortions and incomplete data.

> *God so loved the world that he gave his one and only Son, that whoever believes in him shall not perish but have eternal life.*
>
> John 3:16, NIV

question

What are your strengths?

Most young people, male and female alike, have wished at some point that they had a super power. Superheroes are cool because they can do things that the average person cannot. Superman flies, Flash runs fast, Storm can control the weather, and Iceman can chuck ice at people. Despite all of these powers, the comic universe sees Batman as one of the toughest superheroes to combat. He can even beat Superman because he plays to his strength—his intelligence.

answer

It would be to your advantage to know your strengths so that you can capitalize on them when the time is right. Strengths can come in a variety of forms:

Personality. If you are outgoing, you may be able to encourage and motivate people toward a specific action. You may be good at gathering groups of people. Social people make large functions fun and entertaining. If you are more of a small-group person, you may be best at establishing tight, intimate relationships with others. Each person has a unique personality, so discover what yours is.

Physicality. Every person has a different body type and look. Height, weight, and muscle structure can be to your advantage in a variety of situations. The media idolize the tall, muscular body frame, but this body type is not always the best to have. If you love swimming, you may be better suited to have a slender frame. If you like gymnastics, a smaller frame is required. Each type has advantages.

Intelligence. Some people have a God-given gift for a subject like math or grammar. If you are good with numbers or words, use your gift to help get you ahead.

Innate skills. These skills can help you with people or in your professional life. You can use music, math, and even the ability to paint the Mona Lisa in ketchup in some manner either personally or professionally.

worth thinking about

▶ **Your physicality** and look can help you even if you are not the town beauty. In the field of acting, people who are not conventionally handsome or beautiful fill a variety of character roles.

▶ **Do not hold** your strengths over the heads of those who may not be as good as you are in some way.

▶ **There will likely** always be someone bigger, better, more attractive, and more skilled than you are, but be comfortable in your own skin and know what you do well.

> *Do you see a man skilled in his work? He will stand in the presence of kings. He will not stand in the presence of unknown men.*
> Proverbs 22:29, HCSB

question

What are your weaknesses?

Just as all superheroes have strengths, they also have weaknesses. Superman has kryptonite, and Wolverine knows to stay clear of water since his bones are covered in metal and would likely cause him to sink. No one, not even the Man of Steel, can do everything. You serve yourself well if you know your weaknesses and embrace them. Denying that you have a weakness doesn't make it go away, and it doesn't make you better in that area.

answer

Ignoring weaknesses hampers your progress in other areas, but knowing what they are can help you. Here are some reasons why:

They show you where you can grow. In the Spider-Man story line, Peter Parker does not stop a bad guy because of apathy or fear, and that same man ends up killing his uncle. Due to his weakness, he makes it his goal to be active and help all those in need. He turned a weak point into a strong point. Sometimes a weakness can help you know where to improve.

They show you where not to focus. You cannot change some weaknesses. Daredevil is a blind superhero. He cannot change this fact about himself, so he works on all his other senses. If you are completely tone deaf with zero musical skill, you know not to make a career in music. There is nothing wrong with that. Many successful people fail at one thing only to succeed at another. George Clooney did not make it to professional baseball, but he is one of the most successful actors of recent times.

They show where you need others. Many heroes end up on a team like the Justice League or X-Men, because alone they cannot always defeat the super-villain. If you are a visionary but not a great manager, you know you need someone who can keep finances and paperwork organized. Be receptive to working with people who have skills that you do not.

worth thinking about

▶ **Be open** to growth. If you have weaknesses that you can improve, do not be afraid of working hard to get better.

▶ **Many people** who succeed may not be the most talented, but they are often the hardest working.

▶ **Two heads** are better than one, so if you can develop good relationships with people who complement your talents and shortcomings, you will be ahead of the curve.

> *Our strength grows out of our weaknesses.*
> Ralph Waldo Emerson

72 question

Have you identified your family's unhealthy patterns?

Most families have traditions like going together to cut down a choice Christmas tree each year. Others get together for game night every Friday evening. Some traditions are not as positive as these. As families develop over time, they consistently repeat certain behaviors. To maximize your chances for succeeding in life, identify unhealthy family patterns and then break them.

answer

Unhealthy and destructive family patterns can take a variety of forms. Here are a few examples:

Money. Some families handle money poorly, which causes them to get behind in bills and often into debt. When someone is always playing catch-up, he does not have time to rest. Pressure and tension mount with this type of pattern. Break this pattern, and live a more peaceful life.

Excess. A life of excess can include overeating, alcoholism, addictions to illegal or prescription drugs, and workaholism. In today's society, few people live in moderation. Living in excess creates a topsy-turvy environment and prevents a balanced lifestyle. Eating too much leads to health issues; working too much leads to relational issues; and succumbing to substances makes addiction the focus in life. Substances and extremism do not lead to happiness; rather, they increase the void you are trying to fill.

Conflict. Unhealthy patterns in conflict resolution often take two extreme approaches. One occurs when conflict becomes an explosive event where you hold back no words and physical encounters take place. Another occurs when you avoid conflict and nothing is dealt with. Both of these patterns are not viable options when dealing with conflict. The first leaves loved ones injured emotionally and even physically. The second never brings about resolution and muddies normal communication.

Divorce. The foundation of a healthy family is having two loving parents together, but divorce rips families apart and is harmful to kids. Kids in an intact home tend to do better in school and relationships, according to many studies.

worth thinking about

▶ **Living a life** of excess is like a dog chasing its own tail—you will keep going around but will never get anywhere because you will not get what you want.

▶ **Address conflict** as soon as possible. Avoiding an issue does not make it go away.

▶ **Statistics show** that kids who have two parents in the home end up faring better in life than kids who don't.

> *Those who cannot learn from history are doomed to repeat it.*
> George Santayana

question

What are good habits to have?

A habit is behavior that one repeats so often it eventually becomes involuntary. Some habits are destructive, while others lay a solid foundation for success. While you were in school, taking notes easily became a habit. Because you took notes, you likely fared better than those who did not. Habits are behavioral wrinkles. Each time you make a facial expression, a wrinkle becomes that much more creased into the skin. The more you do something, the more constant it becomes.

answer

A real wrinkle may not be on your list of top desires, but good habits should be. Here are a few you should try to form:

Devotionals. Get in the habit of praying and reading the Bible. By putting God first, you root yourself in truth and satisfy the need you have to stay connected to your Maker.

Study. Even though you are graduating, you should never stop being a student of life. Never think you know it all. If you are interested in certain subjects, then read and research them. Set time aside to dwell on interests you have or subjects that you know you need to be more aware of.

Service. Make time in your life to give to others. This may mean being a big brother or a big sister, tutoring a kid who struggles in school, visiting retirement homes, or helping people in your Bible study get through tough times.

Tithe. If you make a little money, tithe. If you make a lot of money, tithe. Tithing is a habit that helps you place your trust in God. It also indicates your priorities regardless of if you have money or not. Ten percent of your income is typical, but do not be afraid to tithe 15 percent to 20 percent of your income. Ten percent is just the minimum amount.

Workout. Working out can help give you more energy and keep you healthy. Some studies say that working out can even help relieve depression.

worth thinking about

- ▶ **Having good habits** does not guarantee success, but it does put you in a better position for it.

- ▶ **Many who get** more money tithe less. Do not become stingy and possessive of your money. Money, like everything else, is a gift, and God can give it and take it away.

- ▶ **Keeping consistent** devotions is the most important of the habits listed above because it is the fertilizer that helps grow all of the others.

> *We are what we repeatedly do. Excellence then, is not an act, but a habit.*
> Aristotle

question

How do you develop good habits?

Wanting to have good habits is not enough. To want and to do are two very different things. Sentiment is not the same as action, but many people help pacify themselves by thinking of doing good things. However, to be productive you must carry out the appropriate steps to bring about a desired result. Intent plus consistent action equals a change in behavior. Do you know how to develop good habits?

answer

To develop good habits there are three steps you need to take. These steps are as easy as learning your ABC's:

Accountable. Make sure you have someone around to support you in your task of developing good habits. Give that person the authority to correct you and even give rewards and consequences. For instance, if you are trying to get your finances in order, allow that person to keep you on track. If you spend too much, allow your accountability partner to take your credit cards until you can manage them correctly.

Begin now. Start being what you want to be. You have to decide what it is you want to be and then start being it.

Do not hesitate, because today will become tomorrow, tomorrow will turn into next week, and next week will become next month. Before you know it, much time has passed and you have not really changed. It is important to know exactly what your goals are so that you can take specific steps toward those goals.

Consistent. Most people say that if you do something for thirty straight days it becomes a habit. So make this time frame your first goal. Do not take one day off. For thirty days, carry out your desired behavior. If you are trying to enhance your praying habits, set a time each morning when you do your devotionals. Do not just try whenever you have time, because you will either forget or run out of time. Be focused and diligent in honing your habits.

worth thinking about

▶ **Developing good** habits will not be as effective if you do not break bad habits, too. Start by stopping. Stop practicing bad habits and replace them with good ones.

▶ **Try to go** without an undesired habit for thirty days and see if that helps you break free from it.

▶ **Sometimes it is easier** to improve a habit if you do so with a group of people. The synergy that a group effort creates can often be of great support in starting something new.

> *Successful people are successful because they form the habits of doing those things that failures don't like to do.*
> Albert Gray

75

▼

Have you made mistakes in the past?

Some people pretend that they have never done any-thing wrong in their lives. They push the truth so far to the back of their minds they actually convince them-selves that nothing ever really happened. The problem is that when this occurs, nothing gets resolved. Almost every secret is exposed at some point or another. Skeletons eventually escape their closets, and it is bet-ter to deal with them sooner than later.

answer

▼

If you have made mistakes in the past, this is how you need to deal with them:

Forgive yourself. Often the hardest person to forgive is you. This is especially so if you have high standards; it is easy to beat yourself up over bad decisions. If you cannot for-give yourself, you will likely not progress very far in life.

Do not forget. Forgiving is not the same as forgetting. Forgiving allows you to move on, but forgetting minimizes what you have been through. You want to remember so that you do not repeat the same mistakes. Learn as much as you can from your missteps because even though mistakes are painful, repeatedly making mistakes is excruciating.

Move on. Do not keep replaying the events over a million times. Move into a different phase of life. For example, if you were burned in a relationship, do not keep all the photos, the letters, and the special mementos. Those things only remind you of something that went bad. Besides, you should not plan to keep them anyway when you get married. By never moving on, you end up torturing yourself with the hurtful events.

Forgive others. Forgiving is letting go of your right to keep replaying the offense that harmed you. If you do not release others from their offense, then you are the one who gets hurt. Releasing someone of a wrong frees you to move on. Holding on to the wrong increases pain and anger. In the end you are the one harmed, not the offender.

worth thinking about

▶ **Forgiving yourself** does not mean you rationalize what you did and deny that it was wrong. Accept that you made a mistake, and do all you can to avoid repeating it.

▶ **Forgiving someone** who hurt you does not always mean that reconciliation will follow. If someone abused you, or something of that nature, you can forgive that person without reestablishing a relationship.

▶ **If the** relationships can be restored, do all that you can to reconcile differences with those who have hurt you.

> *There is no love without forgiveness,*
> *and there is no forgiveness without love.*
> Bryant H. McGill

76

question

What threats might detour you?

Threats are people or situations that may hinder you in the pursuit of your goals. If you tried out for a spot on a sports team, in a choir, or in a play, you likely had to go up against other people. Competing against others may not have been your only roadblock; you might also have had to overcome your own fears as well. Threats can be real, but they can also be of your own creation due to your fears or apprehensions.

answer

It can be tempting to avoid possible threats because you do not want to get frightened any more than you may already be, but seeing what may lie ahead can also help you plan and better prepare for what is to come. Possible threats include:

Self. Sometimes you may be your own worst enemy. Many individuals never place blame on themselves and instead shirk responsibility and place the guilt on others. However, fear, insecurity, and even pride can lead to failure. Human nature seeks to avoid being caught holding the bag. Perhaps Catherine has major feelings for Nathan, but when he shows interest elsewhere, she tries too hard to change his mind in almost a desperate manner. This only causes him to distance himself even more. In the end, Catherine causes such a fuss that she accuses him of leading her on, when in reality all he did was be nice to her.

Others. There are individuals who do not want you to succeed. They may want the same things as you or perhaps they just don't want you to have what they don't have. Perhaps Kevin wants the same position that you do, so he spreads a rumor to paint you in an inaccurate light.

Bad guy. Just as there is a God who loves and cares for you, there is also a bad guy who seeks to steal, kill, and destroy anything remotely good. The devil does not want you to succeed, and he will stop at nothing to derail you.

worth thinking about

▶ **The harder** you try to place blame elsewhere, the worse it looks on you. If you own up to the mistakes you make, you can minimize many of life's problems.

▶ **You cannot always** stop people from doing bad things to you, but you can control how you handle it. Do not return bad for bad. Do the opposite and show them a kindness they did not show you.

▶ **Stay plugged into** God through prayer and reading the Bible so that when things do get rough, you are better prepared.

> *The thief's purpose is to steal and kill and destroy. My purpose is to give them a rich and satisfying life.*
>
> John 10:10, NLT

What if I just can't let go of a grudge?

Do not judge, or you too will be judged. For in the same way you judge others, you will be judged, and with the measure you use, it will be measured to you.

Matthew 7:1–2, NIV

question
▼
How can your past make a better future?

If you are like the majority of people, you have probably made some mistakes along the way. It is also likely that you have had to endure a difficult situation. Personal failures, family issues, and devastating circumstances are unfortunately a part of life. These occurrences can be deflating and heartbreaking, but they do not have to spell the end of your life. Many times the tough stuff can even better your future.

answer
▼

This does not mean that your past will not hurt; it merely means that there is hope in the midst of pain. Here are a few ways that your past can better your future:

Wisdom. Experience should breed wisdom. By making mistakes you learn how not to do things. As a kid, you thought it might be fun to pick up a bumblebee and play—until you got stung. Then you knew not to mess with a bee again. The same is true if you hung out with the wrong crowd in school and got into trouble. You now know to associate yourself with higher-quality people.

Motivation. Challenging circumstances can build strength. Maybe you did not have a lot of money growing up or you were not as talented as some of the other people you knew. These and other circumstances should motivate you to make a difference and to do something special with your life. Do not let difficulties stop you; let them make you stronger.

Identify. Your story gives you credibility. Perhaps you were abused, slandered, or hurt in some way that not everyone understands. Your story helps you identify with others who have gone through similar situations. You cannot fully understand some things in life unless you go through them personally. Your experience may be the very thing that allows you to connect with a person no one else can reach. Your future may be better because you help make someone else's future better, too.

worth thinking about

▶ Do not repeat mistakes of your past. Once you go past them, move on.

▶ Do not think you know exactly how another feels even if you can relate. Every situation is unique, and each person is different. You cannot know exactly how another person feels about something. Pretending you do only minimizes how the hurt person feels.

▶ Motivation does not equal bitterness. Do not operate out of bitterness and anger.

> *When the going gets tough,*
> *the tough get going.*
> Joseph P. Kennedy

question

▼

Do you know all there is to know?

Since you are a graduate now, you know everything. Right? You have studied, learned, and taken a million tests, so you have to know all there is to know. Don't you? Yet you feel self-pressure because you do not know as much as you think you should. You are no expert at life. The truth is, you are just getting started. You may not be a student taking classes anymore, but you are still a student of life.

answer

▼

At first life can feel like a pop quiz that you are unprepared to take, let alone to pass with excellence. As a graduate, you may even feel as though someone asked you to write a paper on the entire existence of the world and how to live in it, and yet you do not even know where to begin researching. When answering whether you know all there is to know, adopt this L-I-F-E principle:

Less-you-know principle. The older you get, the less you will know. This may seem backward to you because you are supposed to gain wisdom as life goes on, but as time goes by you will learn that there are even more questions than when you first began and that you know fewer of the answers. Getting older is partly coming to grips with the fact that you are a finite being with limited knowledge and understanding.

Invite-answers principle. Do not be afraid to ask other people their thoughts on issues. It is not cool to pretend you know everything simply for the sake of keeping up appearances. Do not download others' beliefs to the hard drive of your heart until you have done your own research, but do not be afraid to ask questions.

Feel fine without answers. You will never be able to answer some questions.

Express answers. When you know what you believe, do not be afraid to express it.

worth thinking about

▶ There is wisdom in being able to admit that you do not know everything.

▶ Those who think they have all the answers are likely the farthest off the mark.

▶ When expressing what you believe, do so with wisdom. You do not want to come off as haughty or to turn anyone off to what you are saying simply because you are being obnoxious.

> *Do you see a man who is wise in his own eyes?*
> *There is more hope for a fool than for him.*
> Proverbs 26:12, HCSB

question

▼

What false beliefs do you hold about yourself?

False beliefs are distortions that you have about yourself. A carnival has a fun house with trick mirrors that make you look distorted. Some make you look tall and slim, and others make you look short and pudgy. False beliefs are like those mirrors. They make you see yourself in a way that is not accurate. False self-concepts can come from friends, family, and even pop culture.

answer

▼

False beliefs can take many forms. You may not think you are smart, attractive, or strong enough. You may think you are a loser, an idiot, or an ugly duckling, but you were not born thinking this. You gave yourself these names, or someone else gave them to you. Many false beliefs fall under two categories:

No one would want you if they knew the real you. This type of false belief makes you conscious of how others perceive you. This is the lie that causes many people to wear masks and prevents them from being authentic. You may feel that you are not attractive to the opposite sex. It is easy to feel isolated, to feel that you are the only one who feels the way you do. The false belief that no one would like the real you hinders you from being honest. In your mind, hiding becomes a better option.

You are not good enough to get the job done. This false belief does not cause you to hide, but it causes you to give up. No matter how hard you try, this lie tells you that you will fail because you are too short, too tall, too weak, too outgoing, too shy, or too whatever else you may think. This lie tells you that whatever you are is the wrong thing for the wrong job at the wrong time. If you want to start an outreach in the inner city, for instance, this lie would tell you that you cannot handle the adversity, that you're the wrong person for the job, and that someone else should do it.

worth thinking about

▶ **People go to extremes** and hide behind personas. When you believe that people would not like the real you, you might dig deeper into a disguise that helps you fit in. This is why some people who want to be different wear the same extreme clothes and live the same extreme lifestyle of those they seek acceptance from.

▶ **When you think** that people do not like the real you, it is tough to feel attractive. Walking with confidence in yourself makes you more attractive.

▶ **Do not buy** into the false lies.

> When your image improves,
> your performance improves.
> Zig Ziglar

question

What do you believe?

In every era, people ask themselves many questions. People long to know more about their existence: What is the meaning of life? Is there life after death? How many licks does it really take to get to the center of a Tootsie Pop? These questions burn inside and beg for an answer. In fact, you spend much of life trying to answer these questions. What you believe about the world determines how you live.

answer

A person's beliefs are central to who he or she is. Having beliefs is important, but you need to avoid two extremes:

Legalism. Legalism is living an extreme doctrine by the letter of a law rather than by the spirit of the intention. If you believe that you are to eat healthy foods, being legalistic would mean never allowing yourself anything that is not the epitome of health, even on special occasions. This mind-set can actually become unhealthy in itself. Legalism also influences a person to hold others to unrealistic expectations as well and generally orders harsh punishments as consequences even in minor cases. Some religions, for instance, have extreme consequences for minor infractions. Grace is low. In cases of legalism, there is often a seed of hypocrisy where the most pious hold others to standards they themselves cannot attain. Legalism focuses so much on minor issues that a participant cannot see the full picture of life.

Relativism. Many of the greatest civilizations fell due to moral decay. Relativism creates a chaotic void of right and wrong. Relativism holds that all ideas are right and wrong if an individual holds them to be true. Where legalism is too narrow, relativism is too broad. This view is so spread out that there is no foundation. A society functioning with this mind-set is doomed for failure because there is no moral absolute. In extreme cases, murder, theft, and worse things are not seen as wrong; rather, they are seen simply as a way of life.

worth thinking about

▶ **On the front end,** relativism may seem attractive because it helps avoid conflict with others, but eventually this leads to more troubles. Where there is no sense of right and wrong, chaos occurs.

▶ **Imagine several children** in a room with no rules. If Billy steals Lindsay's cookies and Tommy pulls Nancy's hair, there would be no consequences because there are no rules.

▶ **Legalism is often** a group's way of holding control over other people.

> *Every man's way is right in his own eyes, but the LORD weighs the hearts.*
> Proverbs 21:2, NAS

question

Why do you believe what you believe?

Every person eventually comes to the point where he or she either embraces or rejects the parents' beliefs. No one should believe something without knowing why. This means that if you have faith, the faith should be yours and not someone else's. Know what you believe and why you believe it.

answer

Christians believe that the Bible is the Word of God, the earth is His creation, and all humanity reflects His image. If you believe in the Bible, then the Scriptures give you many of the why's about what you believe. People do not always know why they believe what they believe. In the Middle Ages, people believed that fog was some über-spiritual event, but they did not know why they believed it. Knowing why you believe what you believe is important because:

Knowing helps combat doubt. Doubt in itself is not always a bad thing; sometimes doubt can help build your faith. When you are unsure of your faith, you need to dig deeper to discover why you believe something. Do not be deflated if you are missing a few answers. Researching answers is a part of maturing. As life goes on, you will meet more and more people who disagree with you. It is important to know why you believe what you believe—many people who disagree with you know why they do not agree with you.

Knowing helps you share your faith. If you get into a discussion about your beliefs and your friend Sharon asks you why you believe something, you cannot rely simply on your feelings. That response will likely not be too effective in convincing her that you have a valid point. Personal experience can be of some help, but it should not be the basis of truth, because every person on earth has a different personal experience. In addition, personal experiences are often misinterpreted.

worth thinking about

▶ **Superstition is not faith**; it is an irrational belief in something based in mysticism and not in truth.

▶ **If you have questions,** write them down and begin to research them as much as you can. Your research will help you build a solid foundation in knowing why you believe what you believe.

▶ **Whatever you do,** do not give up. If you put off your questions, you do yourself as well as those around you a disservice.

> *One person with a belief is equal to a force of ninety-nine who have only interests.*
> John Stuart Mill

82

question

Do you have endurance?

On most freeways on any given day, you can find a few broken-down cars on the side of the road. It does not matter the brand or make of the car if it cannot go anywhere. Many people seek glitz and glamour, but few seek to endure for the long haul. The classic image of the race between the tortoise and the hare illustrates how consistency and hard work will win most of the time.

answer

If you want to be successful in life, you need to develop a strong knack for enduring. Your best friendships will not be the ones where you never fight or argue, but they will be the ones where you are willing to persevere despite your differences. In fact, if there isn't at least a little conflict in a specific relationship, it is likely not all that intimate.

The accomplishments that you take the most pride in are not the ones that come easy. Rather, they are the ones that require a lot of hard work. These peaks in life take blood and tears and a little bit of stubbornness not to give up! You or most people will likely not even remember the goals you reach with little effort. Brett Favre is a future Hall of Fame football player. His statistics are good, especially among quarterbacks. However, people know him best for being the "Iron Man" of football with 117 consecutive starts, breaking the record held by Ron Jaworski. Favre's record may never be broken.

Some people give up because they are tired of failure. However, many give up or at least lose speed once they have reached a certain level of success. When you reach a certain pinnacle of success you might not want to risk failing again, so apathy sets in. Endurance doesn't mean giving it your all just until you succeed; endurance is success itself.

worth thinking about

▶ Enduring is gearing up for the long haul. Do not judge your life merely by one chapter, but rather in its entirety.

▶ It can be easy to lose hope when you cannot see any progress. View success not by goals attained but by your conduct in the pursuit of your goal.

▶ When you have reached a goal, take a moment to set new ones. Do not rest too long on your laurels, because then you become too comfortable and may end up never doing anything else.

> *You need to persevere so that when you have done the will of God, you will receive what he has promised.*
> Hebrews 10:36, NIV

question

Are you loyal?

Loyalty is faithfully committing to a person, group, or cause. In an individual-focused culture, loyalty often takes a backseat to a "what have you done for me lately" mentality. If a romantic relationship is not perfect, simply jump to the next person. If a friend is not cool anymore, find someone else to befriend. If you get bored with a job, simply get a different one. To some, loyalty has gone the way of dial-up Internet.

answer

There are many advantages to being a loyal person. Here are a few reasons why you should seek to be one:

Longevity. When you constantly lack a constant, you are always in transition. You are nearly always just getting started. New beginnings may seem fun, but after a while, you will notice that you struggle to develop depth in any area of your life. It may be fun to start a new relationship, for instance, because of the butterfly feelings and excitement of newness, but if you are always starting over you will not be able to establish an enduring relationship.

Roots. If you never plant yourself anywhere, then the wind of circumstances will easily push you around. You may like to float around and have flexibility in your life, but flexibility should not mean never committing long-term to people or jobs. When tough times occur, you will not have anything to cling to. If tragedy occurs, you will not have people close to you or things to keep your thoughts busy. It is easy to consume yourself with your loss.

Loyalty. If you pledge your loyalty to no one, you will have the loyalty of no one. This creates a lonely and isolating existence. Most jobs come from people you know, so who will get that opening—you or the person who is good friends with the boss? Without loyalty, you are all alone.

worth thinking about

▶ Do not misinterpret change as progress. Constantly starting over is like always starting a race only to stop midway to begin all over.

▶ This does not mean that you should never change jobs. It means that you should give your all to what you are doing and whom you are with.

▶ Being free to do anything you want often means that you do nothing. You cannot expect others to be loyal to you if you are not loyal in turn.

> *Loyalty makes a person attractive.*
> *It is better to be poor than dishonest.*
> Proverbs 19:22, NLT

question

Are you careful of what you say?

"Sticks and stones may break your bones, but words will never hurt you" is a downright lie. In fact, the power of the tongue often does far moredamage than either a stick or a stone. If the power of life and death is in the tongue, it has to be powerful indeed. Do you speak words that build people up? Alternatively, do you speak words to tear them down?

answer

Here are some things to ponder:

Gossip. Gossip is one of the most vicious forms of verbal assassination. By speaking words against others, you are participating in a form of murder against the ones the gossip is about. This can occur in an office or school where someone spreads a rumor. Even if the rumor is true, this does not constitute permission to talk about it. Gossip can also take the form of tabloids or e-mail. Do not participate in these, either. How would you feel if all your personal issues were made public for all to analyze?

Encouragement. Encouragement is building someone up about something that has not yet occurred. Everyone needs to be encouraged to keep on keeping on, so jump at the opportunity to encourage others.

Affirmation. Affirmation is validating that which is already in existence. If someone does a good job or has a specific talent, point out that he or she excels. In a world where criticism is the norm, affirmation is a breath of fresh air.

Flattery. Flattery can appear like affirmation or encouragement, but in actuality, it is a self-serving form of stroking another's ego. Flattery comes about when you want to impress someone or desire recognition from a particular person. Flattery is sucking up to someone to get something in return. Flattery also comes into play when the flatterer wants another to like him. The danger in this is not always the truthfulness of the statement but rather the motivation. You focus affirmation and encouragement on others, but you focus flattery on yourself.

worth thinking about

▶ **Be cautious.** A person who spreads gossip *to* you will likely spread gossip *about* you. Do not share personal information with such people.

▶ **It takes about seven** positive words to negate a negative one, so do not be stingy with your positive words. Many people need to hear them.

▶ **Do not buy** into flattery. A genuine encourager will uplift those below him and those above him as well.

> *Though the tongue is a small part [of the body], it boasts great things. Consider how large a forest a small fire ignites.*
>
> James 3:5, HCSB

question

Are you genuine?

Halloween can be a disconcerting time. Many people around the globe run about in masks, and you cannot be sure what they are like beneath those costumes. On any other day, if a person walked into a bank or store in full costume, most people would likely assume a robbery was in progress. The scary thing is that people wear masks every day, and many times the masks go unnoticed.

answer

Here are a few things that will prevent you from being genuine:

Masks. In Greece, actors would wear masks to indicate what type of character they were playing. As time progressed, not much changed. Masks are deceptive because they show things that are not accurate. Many times people wear masks because they do not like who they really are. Other times they wear masks to hide insecurities or to appear like others. Masks never allow you to be you, and they never allow you to be accepted for the real you.

Walls. Where masks try to show something other than reality, walls attempt to show nothing at all. Walls prevent people from knowing the authentic you. Many times people build walls as a self-defense mechanism. It is not uncommon for a person to live in fear of being hurt if someone is allowed to get too close. If in the past others have hurt your friend Jennifer, it might be tough for her to share private things with you.

Pride. Pride stunts your ability to be genuine simply because pride does not allow you to look bad. For example, if Dan fails his physics test, he may not tell anyone that he bombed the test. He does not want to lose his reputation as the smart one. Pride is an intentional effort to look better than you are.

worth thinking about

▶ **Being genuine** does not mean sharing everything about yourself; it is simply avoiding an intentional attempt to hide who you are.

▶ **Being genuine also** does not mean that you cannot be colorful. Having a diverse personality is not the same as wearing a mask to cover what you are. Some who are colorful hide it to look more responsible.

▶ **The problem** with walls is that they not only can protect you, they also can imprison you.

> *Honesty and transparency make you vulnerable. Be honest and transparent anyway.*
> Mother Teresa

Can money bring happiness?

Money never made a man happy yet, nor will it. There is nothing in its nature to produce happiness. The more a man has, the more he wants. Instead of its filling a vacuum, it makes one.

Benjamin Franklin

question

Do you honestly love people?

The Love Chapter (1 Corinthians 13) is one of the most beloved works of the Bible. It outlines the importance, nature, and eternal value of love. However, it also holds the key to the most important principle in the teachings of Paul. The principle is that no matter what good things you do or accomplishments you attain, if you do not love others then none of it matters.

answer

The following is a checklist of the attributes of love:

Patient. Be patient with others just as you want others to be patient to you.

Kind. Be gentle and nice to people. A smile can go a long way. Raising your voice to yell at someone almost never causes the other person to listen better. In most cases, a person shuts down and ceases to listen when someone is yelling at him.

Not jealous. Do not desire what others have, but be joyful when others succeed.

Does not brag. Love is others-focused, but bragging puts attention back on you. Allow others to build you up, and put your focus on affirming others.

Does not demand its own way. Do not always demand that you do things your way all the time.

Not irritable. Do not make others have to walk on eggshells when they are around you.

Holds no record of wrongs. Do not keep score so that you can bring up past mistakes in order to prove your point. Forgiving is letting go of an offense.

Righteous. Do the right thing at the right time the right way. Base your love in integrity.

Seeks truth. Love seeks truth and not simply assumptions based on emotions or false beliefs.

Bears all things. Love covers mistakes and does not seek to expose fragilities to everyone for personal gain. Love desires to protect others.

worth thinking about

- ▶ **Love shares** and does not try to hoard everything for oneself. Love puts others first.

- ▶ **Do not become** cynical to the point that you are skeptical of everyone. Do not make people have to prove themselves continually. Believe the best of people, and give the benefit of the doubt.

- ▶ **Love does not** give up. Love is consistent and lasting. Love is a decision and not simply a feeling.

> *If I give all my possessions to feed the poor,*
> *and if I surrender my body to be burned,*
> *but do not have love, it profits me nothing.*
> 1 Corinthians 13:3, NAS

87

Can you lead?

Many people look at a leader as simply a charismatic figurehead who starts a movement through words and passion. Charisma and vision can be important roles in leadership; however, these qualities are not the only aspects of leadership. One key aspect of leadership often ignored is leading by example. Many leaders can get people revved up with a speech, but fewer actually practice what they preach. Can you lead by example?

answer

You cannot teach some aspects of leadership. You cannot teach personality or passion. However, you can improve on leading by example. There are many definitions of what leadership is. Basically, leadership is the ability to influence others to action. There are many types of leaders. Some lead loudly, some lead quietly, but the best lead by example. Even if you are quiet, shy, and timid, you can lead by example. Seek to go the extra mile and do the things that others do not want to do. Others might just follow your example. By being a pacesetter, you can influence others to take action, so by definition you become a leader. Mother Teresa never ran a Fortune 500 company, but she was an example of how to be self-sacrificing. Many have followed her example, and few people would argue that she was not a leader in her own right.

You cannot control other qualities you possess, so capitalize on this one. If you determine to set the example, you will have the opportunity to lead others by setting the example. The question is not whether you *can* lead, but rather *if* you will lead. This means that it may not be easy. In fact, you may have to work twice as hard as anyone else has to. But if you want something bad enough, you will go the distance. Even if you have natural leadership ability, make it a goal to lead by example rather than by words.

worth thinking about

▶ Be sure to lead toward the right things. Strong and effective leaders have led others to horrible ends, so be a good leader and lead others to good ends.

▶ Leading by example can entail working harder than anyone else does, but in the midst of hard work, do not neglect relationships. Work harder at those, too.

▶ Do not let your age discourage you from setting an example. Timothy in the Bible was a leader, and he led through his actions.

> *Let no one look down on your youthfulness, but rather in speech, conduct, love, faith and purity, show yourself an example of those who believe.*
>
> 1 Timothy 4:12, NAS

88

question

▼

Are you humble?

Pride is having an unrealistic concept of one's own importance, ability, or influence. Being humble is to be modest about one's own self-importance. Humility is self-confidence in its purest form. Having your own self-importance in check is vital for your future. Having confidence is good, but walking in pride is not. People do not like to be around others who are self-centered.

answer

▼

Humility is the opposite of being a weak person. Humility is having strength and keeping it under control. The most powerful people are not those who flaunt their power; rather, they are those who could flaunt but instead withhold. Many people promote themselves to a degree that does not accurately reflect their true abilities. Many politicians are great on television. They tell the public to choose them because they will bring change and are the best option, but do their actions back up their ability to carry through the promises they make?

The most impressive are typically those who do not boast of their abilities. Cal Ripken Jr. is the Iron Man of baseball. His record of consecutive games played will likely go unmatched for a long time. The day he decided to sit out, he did not make a big deal about it. He simply did not play. Everyone was shocked not to see Cal play. It instantly became headline news, because when a person does something great many times, others will boast of it so you do not have to. It is better to let others praise your work rather than you. It is harder to praise self-promoters because they do it for themselves.

Seek to be a humble person. Pride does indeed come before the fall. CEOs, athletes, and even some ministers hold themselves in higher regard than they should, only to fall back down to earth because of scandal, failure, or simply not getting the job done.

worth thinking about

▶ The higher someone seeks to make himself, the farther he has to fall, so do not try to make yourself greater than you are.

▶ To walk in pride hampers one's ability to hear feedback from others. When someone has a high opinion of his or her own opinions, it is difficult to accept the opinions of others as valuable.

▶ Those who are humble attract the attention of God and gain His favor.

> *A person's pride will humble him,*
> *but a humble spirit will gain honor.*
> Proverbs 29:23, HCSB

question

Do you strive for excellence?

At work and in everyday life you will meet people who simply live to get by. They do the least amount of work possible. This is a mentality entrenched in mediocrity. Some people want to do great things but never put forth the effort to do something tremendous. To walk in excellence is not only to put your best foot forward but also to do so with consistency.

answer

Excellence is not simply doing something great, but it is doing the best you can possibly do. Many talented people do great jobs, but they rarely do their best. Do not rest on your talent alone to get you by. Even if your work looks better than the work of others, you know if you have done your best. Excellence is a mentality and not simply a result. If Tara is a gifted musician who spends only five minutes doing what takes other people hours to do, this does not mean Tara did so with excellence. What might Tara come up with if she invested hours into her work? Do not live by the standards of others, but shoot for higher goals.

To see someone work with a mediocre mentality, you need only remember the last time you had to wait in a long line only to face an unfriendly individual behind the counter. Customer service is not what it used to be. When was the last time you remember getting excellent service? Many workers stick to their basic job descriptions and meet any request beyond the basics with sighs and shrugs. Good service has become the exception and not the norm.

Walking in excellence means putting forth a product that is comparable to other options. If you are recording an album, you do not want to put out junk because no one will buy it. You need to do the project the right way without cutting corners. Excellence gives credibility to your worldview. Poor workmanship equals a weak message.

worth thinking about

▶ **Excellence gives credibility** to your beliefs. If you film a movie and do it well, the message within the movie has a higher level of believability.

▶ **Poor work weakens** your worldview. If you make questionable business decisions and people know you are a person of faith, they will doubt not only you but also your faith.

▶ **Excellence is contagious.** By setting higher standards, those around you will likely raise their self-expectations and efforts.

> *Lazy people are soon poor;*
> *hard workers get rich.*
> Proverbs 10:4, NLT

90

Are you generous?

Few countries give as much money to special causes as America does. America funds several mission and community organizations around the globe. Many people argue that this is the reason America is such a rich country. The biblical principle that you reap what you sow is based in the concept of generosity. This thought holds that when you give to others, you receive in return. Are you a generous person?

answer

If you are generous, you likely do the following:

Actually give. Wanting to give is not enough; the act of giving shows a generous heart. In a capitalistic society, many people focus on gaining money rather than giving it out, but being generous places value on helping others. Giving does not have to be limited to money. Being generous could be giving a young worker extra training and helping him climb the corporate ladder. If the corporate CEO sees a young worker who has a lot of potential, she may be able to open doors to him that he would not otherwise know about.

Joyfully give. If Jim is a corporate bigwig and he gives out of duty but does so while gritting his teeth, his giving is in vain. In the end, the act of giving is beneficial only for those who actually enjoy giving.

Give more. If you make a lot of money or have a lot of influence, more is required of you. To whom much is given, much more is required. This may not seem fair, but neither is a single mom living in poverty while other moms live in luxury. A custodian does not have the resources of a millionaire who has much more to offer.

Give other ways. Maybe money is not what you need to give. For some, money is the easiest to give. Giving time, resources, and advice is often more helpful to those in need.

worth thinking about

▶ **Being generous** may include not hiding yourself in comfortable hiding places. It takes effort to make phone calls and talk to people.

▶ **Being generous** may also be interacting with people whom you would not normally interact with. You may not feel comfortable with the elderly, but do not waste your time only with those you are comfortable with.

▶ **When you give,** do not announce it to the world. Giving should be selfless, and some do so only to get recognition.

Give freely and become more wealthy;
be stingy and lose everything.
Proverbs 11:24, NLT

question
Do you share credit?

In school there are often social hierarchies that dictate one's popularity status. These ranking systems create a competitive environment where it is difficult to share anything, let alone credit. Winning homecoming queen or the weekend's ball game can give you a social boost, so it may be unwise to share the limelight with those with whom you are competing. This competitive nature does not lessen beyond school because much more is at stake than social status.

answer

There is a tendency to get as much credit as possible to gain favor and acceptance in the real world, too. You may want a raise, a career change, or even more social influence, so competition can breed self-interest. Resist this urge. Instead, do the opposite. If you are on a team and you do a good job, highlight how well others did. This does not mean you should lie or give them credit for work that you did. It simply means to identify good work when it occurs.

When you share credit, others are more open to giving you credit. It helps lower the competitive wall and helps you work better as a team. For example, star basketball players frequently take primary credit for their team's success. One famous athlete credits his teammates by thanking them for helping *him* win. When a player has a strong sense of entitlement and believes he is the team, other players secretly get annoyed. This can lead to a toxic team environment.

When you do not share credit, others will eventually get tired of working with you. If you are working on a public relations campaign and Michelle and Bennett give you some great ideas, it is important to let the bosses know that they were influential in your effort. If you do not, your coworkers will be less willing to offer ideas next time around. Many times people do not share credit because of personal insecurities, but this can sabotage a career if you are not careful.

worth thinking about

- ▶ **Trying to hoard** all of the credit is a shortsighted move. To have a long-lasting career, it is vital to share credit with those around you.

- ▶ **It will be difficult** to find team players if you are not one as well.

- ▶ **Be sure to affirm** people publicly and privately. When a worker does a good job, tell others in front of him, and do so one-on-one as well.

> *Give credit where credit is due.*
> Author Unknown

question

▼

What do you do with romantic ties?

Preparing for a job and dealing with the logistics of transition may be the least of your worries. If you have a special someone on your arm, you may have no idea what to do in this next phase of life. Life is full of major decisions, but only a few are bigger than choosing a course of action with someone you are in a romantic relationship with.

answer

▼

Romantic ties can be sources of joy and energy, but they might also lead down a path of heartache and despair. Here are some things you have to consider:

Marriage material. You have to be honest in figuring this out. Is the person you are with someone you could see yourself marrying? If not, do not waste your time. The just-hanging-out-for-the-heck-of-it date does not turn out too well.

Circumstances. What are your future circumstances? If you are moving for a job or for your education, consider whether the two of you can endure a long-distance relationship. In most cases, long-distance relationships do not work. If you know already that the relationship will not work, break it off immediately. There is no use in stretching it out and prolonging the inevitable. If you want to make a romantic relationship work long-distance, you need to plan how you can get this done. Plan how you will deal with visits and holidays. Distance can make hearts grow fonder. Persistent absence, however, makes the will weak.

Good decisions. If you have major doubts, do not rush anything. The last thing you want to do is make a mistake that will stay with you the rest of your life. There is no harm in giving a situation time to work itself out. However, if you know you want to be together, the circumstances permit it, and you have the support of those around you, do not be afraid to take action.

worth thinking about

▶ **If you decide** to end a relationship, be sensitive to the heart of the person with whom you are breaking up. You can cause emotional scarring to someone you care about if you are callous or flippant.

▶ **Do not forget** to look at your income. If you cannot afford living now, you will not be able to afford it any better if you marry.

▶ **If you believe** that the person you are romantically involved with is the one you are to marry, then include him or her in your decision making about the future.

> ▼
> *No reason to stay is a good reason to go.*
> Author Unknown

93

How do you look for a future spouse?

Choosing a spouse is not always as easy as the movies would have you believe. There are a multitude of possibilities and outcomes depending on whom you end up with and how you go about getting together. If you have come to a place in your life where you really want to get married, it is as important to do it the right way as it is to marry the right person.

answer

Picking a mate is not like taking a multiple-choice test in sociology class, so do your best to get it right:

Core beliefs. It is imperative that you marry someone who shares the same views on faith, God, and family. Your core beliefs must be congruent with your spouse's. If they are not, you are playing Russian roulette with your children's futures, because they will grow up in a home of division and confusion.

Where to look. The best place to look is at church. Not all people who go to church share your values, but you have a better chance there than at a local bar or on the Internet. If you have a bad record of accomplishment in relationships, look at where you met your past romances.

If you typically met them at a party, you should not be surprised at the outcome. If you want a long-lasting and in-depth relationship, go to a place that promotes these same qualities.

Do things the right way. If you find a good candidate, try to do things the right way. Show each other respect, do not push sexual boundaries, and be sure to keep God first.

Allow input. Allow people you trust, like friends, pastors, and parents, to speak to your relationship. Isolating yourselves from everyone else is dangerous. You are not always in your right mind when you feel all lovey-dovey, so get input from those who are more objective. Many times others can see issues you may not.

worth thinking about

▶ Sex before marriage can ruin a relationship. The two of you may be a great fit, but crossing those boundaries can lead to trust issues and even depression.

▶ A good idea is for the man to first ask permission from the woman's father. In this way, he shows respect and honor to the father.

▶ If the other person does not want to involve family, it might be a red flag. Your spouse's family will play a significant role in your future, so scout the prospective in-laws.

> *The man who finds a wife finds a treasure, and he receives favor from the LORD.*
> Proverbs 18:22, NLT

question
▼
How can serving others change your life?

There are different phases of life, and some are more black and white than others. You may have no idea what to do next, but you do not have to have all the answers. When you do not know what to do, see who around you does know. If someone else is doing something interesting, try to help him out in his efforts.

answer
▼

There is nothing wrong in serving someone else's vision if you do not know what else to do. In fact, it should be a prerequisite to serve someone else's vision before you ask others to serve yours. In the Bible, David was serving cheese to his brothers when he became acquainted with Goliath. Serving others can sometimes lead you directly to your destiny. David took care of Goliath and earned the favor of God and a nation. Take time to look around and see whom you can follow. What are your options?

Serve those who need help. Many people need you to take care of them and invest in their lives. Gideon was working hard when he got a call to lead an army. Gideon was the lowest in his family, his family was the lowest in his area, and yet his serving attitude opened doors for him to lead an entire army.

Serving others can give perspective in life that will pave the road for your future. Joseph kept rising to prominence because of his servant attitude. Even when a false accusation of sexual indiscretion threatened his future, he still became successful. People betrayed Joseph more than once, but eventually Joseph's diligence paid off. He became the second-most-powerful man in Egypt. Serving others may not sound all that invigorating, but it can be more rewarding than many other qualities. When you serve, people eventually take notice, and some people will even want to help you.

worth thinking about

▶ **Serving others** is a maturing process, because it helps you focus on them rather than on yourself.

▶ **Serving someone** else's vision should not be because you are afraid to branch out on your own. Safety and security should not be the sole motives for serving another.

▶ **Be sure to check** your motives for what you do. Do not seek to serve only influential people; seek also to serve those who are considered nobodies.

> *Do you see any truly competent workers? They will serve kings rather than working for ordinary people.*
> Proverbs 22:29, NLT

95

Why should you look into mission work?

Missions involve going to a specific people group and sharing the love of God with them. A mission trip often has a particular focus, such as medical access, building construction, or drama ministry. Typically, missions are in a different country, but there are some efforts even in the United States. If you have no idea what to do, open yourself to the possibility of doing some mission work.

answer

Here are a few reasons why you should consider this:

Selflessness. Mission work is a form of serving others. This type of experience can help you become more others-focused and less you-centered. Being free and independent is a great gift, but sometimes it is good to see how others live to appreciate that gift. Many people never get to experience the joy of putting others before self.

Skills. If you join a mission team that utilizes an area of interest you have, you may also be able to hone your skills as well. If you have medical experience and go on a medical mission trip, you can use those skills. Perhaps you are a performer; if so, joining a drama mission trip could be twice as attractive for you because you can help others and perform, too.

Finances. You may have no money, but it is normal for someone going on a mission trip to raise support from loved ones or from fund-raisers. If you join a nonprofit mission group, all the donations you get are tax-deductible. This is attractive to potential givers.

Options. If you have no idea what to do, a mission trip is a good option. By going to another country, you can gain insight into a different culture. Exposure to such differences can have a transforming effect on you. More than one young person has come home more mature and more focused.

worth thinking about

▶ **Doing mission work** can look good on a résumé, especially if the prospective employer values community service. At the very least, it shows that you are a team player and have a servant's heart.

▶ **Mission trips also** give you a chance to travel to countries and meet people you might not otherwise be able to see in a lifetime.

▶ **Even if you** do not get a clearer picture of your long-term future on a mission trip, the worst thing that happens is that you help people and get to travel.

> *You will be my witnesses in Jerusalem, and in all Judea and Samaria, and to the ends of the earth.*
> Acts 1:8, NIV

question

Who is responsible?

answer

We must reject the idea that every time a law's broken, society is guilty rather than the lawbreaker. It is time to restore the American precept that each individual is accountable for his actions.

Ronald Reagan

question

How do you avoid doing nothing?

When life transitions, sometimes you are left with no idea of what to do. Graduation will not be the last time you question whether you should take a right or go left, but you can start a good pattern by determining not to simply do nothing. "Nothing" can take many forms, but it often includes lots of TV, the Internet, or some other form of mindless entertainment along with fast food. Living vicariously through people on TV is not truly living.

answer

Do not be caught up in media overload and then confuse it with doing something productive. To avoid doing nothing, try these ideas:

Get active. When you have nothing else to do, the least you can do is get in good shape. Working out helps you feel better and can assist in giving you some sense of meaning and purpose.

Keep a journal. Take time a couple of days a week to go to a coffee shop or the beach to write about your thoughts and events. Keep track of the people in your life and the progress of your life. This helps keep your mind and heart sharp and active. It can also give you a record of events that you can look back at and chart your life as it progressed in that season.

Go on a road trip. Get a group of friends together and go on a road trip some place. The modern generation often judges their existence by their experiences, so create a good memory by boldly going where you have never gone before. Take the trip and cherish it. A road trip in and of itself does not hold answers to your future, but it might help you see things from a different perspective.

Try something new. When nothing to do presents itself, take a shot at something you might not normally do. Submit some of your writing to a publisher, apply to a culinary school, or try your hand at stocks. Pick something that intrigues you, and give it a shot.

worth thinking about

▶ **When writing**, instead of tossing around mundane facts, write poems or short stories.

▶ **Do not feel** that you have to take people on your road trip. There are times in life when you need to think on your own, so if that time is now, do not worry about heading out by yourself.

▶ **You might also** want to put more time into a hobby you have by taking a painting class or even joining a local sports team so you can have social interaction at the same time.

> *If a man is lazy, the rafters sag;*
> *if his hands are idle, the house leaks.*
> Ecclesiastes 10:18, NIV

97

question
▼
What are the consequences of being lazy?

The worst thing in the world after graduation is not being clueless about your future—it is doing absolutely nothing. Do not allow the unknown to become apathy. Apathy turns into laziness, and before you know it forty years have passed and you are not altogether different than you are now.

answer
▼

When you allow yourself to slip into laziness, you open the doors to a variety of consequences that can be highly detrimental:

Open self to sin. King David in the Bible is a clear illustration of what can happen when one becomes lazy. In the season when he should have been with his army, he instead found himself watching a beautiful married woman. He had her husband killed and committed adultery. When a person is not active in what he should be, it is easy to slip into temptation. Keeping oneself busy helps distract from possible unsavory deterrents.

Lose momentum. Life can sometimes be like an uphill hike, and when you stop, you sometimes lose momentum. By doing nothing, it becomes more and more difficult to start over again. When you take major detours, you can also become insecure in your ability to keep on going. When you have not used your skills in a while, it is easier to doubt what you are capable of doing. Idleness is one of the major reasons for mediocre expectations.

Desensitize self. After living a while in a particular environment, a person eventually gets used to it. When you live in a state of nothingness and people who know nothing surround you, it becomes the norm. Hope and faith go out the window if there seems to be no way out of your current circumstances. Keep going and do not give up, because giving up makes it more difficult to start again. Keep dreaming and keep hoping, because allowing yourself to become apathetic and then lazy is a road that leads nowhere.

worth thinking about

▶ **Keeping yourself busy** is different from busying yourself. The latter is an all-consuming state of unrest. The former is keeping yourself sharp and prepared for the next step.

▶ **The longer you** wait, the harder it is to keep going. If you have already lost momentum, start again now. Do not wait any longer.

▶ **There is no existence** worse than one without hope. Keep yourself optimistic, and keep trying. Fight off temptations to give up.

> *There is surely a future hope for you,*
> *and your hope will not be cut off.*
> Proverbs 23:18, NIV

question

Do you know how to eat healthy?

Keeping yourself healthy should top your list of things to do after graduation because it can prolong your life and increase your quality of life. In a world of easy-access food, it is all too common to eat out of convenience rather than health. Some people do not know how to eat healthy while others just choose not to. Do not take the easy way out; make eating wisely a part of your lifestyle.

answer

When you do not know what else to do with your life, the least you can do is take care of the basics in a wise manner. Here are some suggestions:

Say good-bye to fast food. Fast food is, normally, bad to eat; it is surprising that so many people consume it every day. Many times even the "healthy" options are not healthy at all. Many salads are chock-full of sugar and fat. Many places offer a few healthy options, so order carefully. You can check most franchise restaurants online to see the nutrition counts of their menu items.

Organic food. Many otherwise healthy products in stores are still processed and not as good for your system. Many wheat and dairy products contain extra preservatives to prolong shelf life. Try to replace your current menu with organic possibilities. This is especially true with fruits, veggies, and meats. You may also want to buy organic eggs. Read labels to know what you are eating. As a rule, if you cannot pronounce it, you might not want to eat it.

Balanced diet. The United States Department of Agriculture (USDA) has developed a food pyramid that gives the right balance of foods for proper nutrition. Select choices from each of the categories, more to less, in this order: grains, vegetables, fruits, milk, and meats and beans. Couple exercise or physical activity with your diet, and stay within your body's calorie needs.

worth thinking about

▶ Check out the USDA pyramid at mypyramid.gov and develop a personal meal plan.

▶ Avoid or eat sparingly processed meats like sandwich meat you buy in packets. These types of meats may be linked to certain kinds of cancers.

▶ Eat with other people. Use mealtime as a good time to catch up with others. People who eat together are healthier than those who do not.

> *We think fast food is equivalent to pornography, nutritionally speaking.*
> Steve Elbert

question

Do you know how to stay healthy?

To stay healthy you need to do more than just eat right. To eat right only and not exercise is like writing notes for your class but never taking time to memorize them in order to use the information for a practical purpose. People drive cars and take elevators a lot these days, so people do not get the amount of exercise they might have a few decades ago.

answer

Staying in good shape has positive effects on your life, so here are some ways to get started on being healthy:

Work out. To stay healthy, working out is a necessity. Be sure to have a balanced workout. Do not do only the things you do well. Some people do mostly weights, and other people do mostly cardiovascular activities. It is important to do both cardio and weights. If you want to lose body fat, you will want to do cardio, but if you want to gain strength, you will want to do more weights. Whatever you decide, do not just do one or the other.

Consistent. Be consistent in your exercising. Work out at least three times a week no matter what. This may mean planning if special events get in the way. Plan to work out at least twenty minutes, but try to get to where you can work out between an hour and an hour and a half. You may want to find a partner to help keep you exercising.

Activities. Try adding active things to do. If you like the outdoors, plan a hike on weekends. If you like sports, get on a team. Perhaps you can conduct work meetings while golfing or after playing racquetball. Take the stairs instead of the elevator. Another option is to park farther away than you normally would to get some walking in at work. You can also use your lunchtime to eat and then take a walk.

worth thinking about

▶ **Staying healthy** can help you increase your confidence. When you feel good about yourself, you feel good about your health. It can help build you up.

▶ **Working out** at least forty-five minutes a day has shown to improve some individual's mental health.

▶ **Disciplining yourself** in the health arena can help you in disciplining other areas of your life as well. If you can handle your health better, it might help with money, schedules, and relationships.

> *Leave all the afternoon for exercise and recreation, which are as necessary as reading. I will rather say more necessary because health is worth more than learning.*
> Thomas Jefferson

100   question

▼

When is it time to try something new?

Hope is a rare commodity in life, and many people give up too soon. Yet there is a time when you may want to think about trying something different. It is vital that you do not give up but instead simply change your focus. Maybe you wanted to paint, and that fell through, but some people may seek you out to design Web sites. Giving up is losing hope; changing focus is taking advantage of opportunities right in front of you.

answer

▼

If you do not know when it is a good time to make a change, here are some suggestions:

Five-year plan. It is important to be willing to give any plan at least five years to be established. If you cannot invest that amount of time, you might not want to try it. However, if after five years you have tried everything you can and there is little to no progress, you might want to consider something new. If your heart is to be a professional singer and people are not asking you to sing at events or on their CDs, after five years it is okay to look elsewhere.

Other interests. Be aware of other interests that present themselves during this five-year time. If after five years nothing has taken off in your original plan, you might be able to have a backup plan. Harrison Ford did carpentry work to pay the bills before George Lucas asked him to read for Han Solo in *Star Wars*.

Life changes. Life will change, and when it does, your decisions will change. When you have a family, it is important to put them first. If you are a businessperson, you may not be able to travel as much as you once did. Never sacrifice family for profit. Do not view investing in family as failure in other areas of life. Many families are dysfunctional. By having a strong, committed, and loving family, you accomplish something that many never do.

worth thinking about

- ▶ If after five years you are making progress, keep trying. Five years is a good benchmark to be able to see progress and not necessarily complete fruition.

- ▶ Do not switch your focus, continually chasing a dream only to change it twelve times for something else.

- ▶ Family is not an excuse to ignore all chances. If there is a great job offer, you have the means to do it, and you have your spouse's support, do not fear taking a risk.

> *Make the best use of what is in your power, and take the rest as it happens.*
> Epictetus

Readers who enjoyed this book will also enjoy

100 Answers to 100 Questions About Being a Great Dad

100 Answers to 100 Questions About Being a Great Mom

100 Answers to 100 Questions About God

100 Answers to 100 Questions About God's Promises

100 Answers to 100 Questions About Loving Your Husband

100 Answers to 100 Questions About Loving Your Wife

100 Answers to 100 Questions About Prayer

100 Answers to 100 Questions to Ask Before You Say "I Do"